IDEAS FOR GREAT
PATIOS & DECKS

By the Editors of Sunset Books and Sunset Magazine

Soothing hot tub holds center stage on detached garden deck.

LANDSCAPE ARCHITECT: JAMES BRADANINI, BRADANINI & ASSOCIATES

Sunset Books Inc. ■ **Menlo Park, California**

Book Editor
Scott Atkinson

Coordinating Editors
Suzanne Normand Eyre
Kevin Freeland

Design
Joe di Chiarro

Illustrations
Bill Oetinger

Photo Styling
JoAnn Masaoka Van Atta

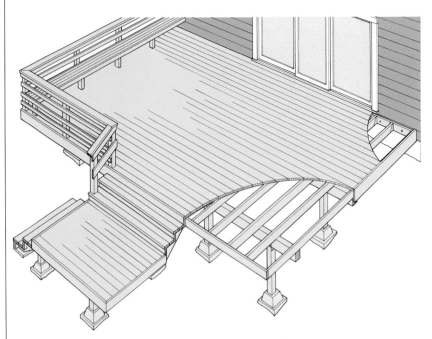

Typical deck design employs evenly spaced structural members below the surface lumber. For details, see page 19.

Photographers
Scott Atkinson: 27, 59 right, 71;
Glenn Christiansen: 32 bottom, 57
bottom, 84–85 bottom; **Peter
Christiansen:** 36 bottom, 63, 88–89
bottom; **Crandall & Crandall:** 44 top
center, 47 bottom right, 51 left, 54
bottom, 56 left, 69 left, 78 right;
Stephen Cridland: 35 bottom left, 49
top right, 55 right; **Mark Darley:** 30;
W. B. Dewey: 61 right; **Derek Fell:** 31
bottom, 43 top; **Jay Graham:** 28
bottom, 48; **Philip Harvey:** 1, 4, 5,
6–7,13, 14, 21, 22–23, 24, 26, 28 top, 29,
32 top, 33, 36 top, 38, 39, 40 top left
and bottom, 41, 42, 43 bottom, 44 top
left, 45, 46 left and right, 47 bottom
left, 49 bottom, 50, 51 right, 52, 53, 54
top, 56 right, 58 bottom, 62 right,
64–65, 66, 67, 69 bottom right, 70, 75,
77, 79, 82, 85 top, 86, 87 bottom, 89
top, 90, 92, 95; **David Livingston:** 91
bottom right; **Jack McDowell:** 76;
Richard Nicol: 44 bottom, 68, 83 top,
91 top right; **Don Normark:** 25 right,
81 top, 83 bottom, 87 top; **Jerry Pavia:**
72 top; **Norman A. Plate:** 35 top and
bottom right, 40 top right, 58 top, 78
left; **Chad Slattery:** 57 top, 91 left;
K. Bryan Swezey: 74; **Michael S.
Thompson:** 31 top, 44 top right, 59 left,
73 top; **Brian Vanden Brink:** 37;
Darrow M. Watt: 72–73; **Western
Wood Products Association:** 69 top
right; **Peter O. Whiteley:** 25 left, 34, 46
center, 47 top, 49 top left, 55 left; **Russ
Widstrand:** 60; **Tom Wyatt:** 62 left,
80–81 bottom, 94.

All Decked Out

This first outdoor addition to *Sunset*'s popular *"Ideas For Great..."* series is crammed full of ideas and information to help you dream, then design the patio or deck of your choice.

More than 130 photos show the latest in landscapes, from tiny garden retreats of rustic brick to sweeping, multilevel decks in redwood and mahogany. Clear examples allow you to review the latest offerings in flagstone, pavers, and concrete tints and textures. When you're ready to dig in, you can also take advantage of a solid introduction to patio planning.

Many landscaping professionals, manufacturers, and homeowners shared ideas with us or allowed us to photograph their installations. We'd especially like to thank Artistic Tile, City Lights, Deckmaster, Dietters Water Garden, Illumination Sales Corporation, Menlo Park Hardware, Tile Visions, and Alan Masaoka.

Special thanks go to Marcia Williamson for carefully editing the manuscript and to Stephen Zusy for assisting with photo scouting.

Cover: A shady, secluded patio features rectangular slate tiles laid in an even grid, with matching grout. Note how tiles are cut around accent boulders. Landscape architect: Louis J. Marano. Cover design by Vasken Guiragossian. Photography by Philip Harvey. Photo styling by JoAnn Masaoka Van Atta.

Editorial Director, Sunset Books:
Bob Doyle

Fourth printing December 1997

CONTENTS

DECK, PATIO, OR BOTH?   4

A PLANNING PRIMER   7
What Are Your Options? ▪ How's Your Weather?
Making a Base Map ▪ Code Concerns
Experimenting with Your Ideas ▪ Patio Profiles
Deck Details ▪ Formalizing Your Plan
Can You Do It Yourself?

GREAT PATIOS & DECKS   23
The Low-level Deck ▪ Wraparounds
Coping with Slopes ▪ An Air of Detachment
Small-space Strategies ▪ Up-front Ideas
Inside Out ▪ Pool Platforms ▪ Spas & Hot Tubs
Up on the Roof ▪ Decisive Steps
Railings & Other Detailing ▪ Sitting Pretty
Overhead Options ▪ Gazebos ▪ Storage Solutions
The Outdoor Kitchen ▪ Planters & Pockets
Garden Meets Patio ▪ A Splash of Water

A SHOPPER'S GUIDE   65
Lumberyard Primer ▪ Brick ▪ Concrete
Concrete Pavers ▪ Ceramic Tile ▪ Stone
Loose Materials

INDEX   96

SPECIAL FEATURES
Tools of the Trade **13** ▪ Guides to Good Design **14**
Choosing Structures **16** ▪ Choosing Amenities **17**
Working with Professionals **21**
A Guide to Garden Pools **75**
Adobe: A Touch of the Old Southwest **87**
Lighting up the Night **92**

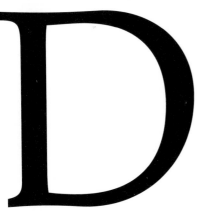

DECK, PATIO, OR BOTH?

In the quest for living space, there's one spot we sometimes overlook: outside. What better way to take the heat off interior traffic, bring the outdoors in, and frame dramatic vistas than to build or expand an outdoor hardscape?

Today's homeowner has plenty of options. Your outdoor room might be classic and formal or fluid and naturalistic. You may be yearning for a remote private refuge, a sheltered dining alcove, a restorative spa or simply for a flat spot for sunbathing and stargazing. Or maybe you want it all. You needn't settle for that boring patio slab. New materials, shapes, and amenities abound.

First things first: would you prefer a patio or deck? Sometimes

Pipe railing and diagonally laid mahogany decking create sleek contemporary-looking setting.

LANDSCAPE DESIGNER: MICHAEL GLASSMAN/ENVIRONMENTAL CREATIONS, INC.

it's simply a matter of site or style. Deck lumber is durable and resilient underfoot, and it does not store heat the way other materials can. And because it's available in a wide range of species, grades, and sizes, wood adapts easily to individual budgets and architectural styles. Depending on the effect you desire, you can let your deck weather naturally or you can seal or stain it.

Patios, on the other hand, lend a sense of permanence and tradition to a formal garden or house design. You might choose unit masonry—traditional brick, ceramic tile, or elegant stone. Concrete pavers, especially interlocking types, are rising stars, and they're easy for the do-it-yourselfer to install. And don't rule out concrete; you'll discover there are lots of jazzy techniques for coloring, texturing, and softening the familiar slab. Loose materials are yet another option.

Technically speaking, you'll find that the choice of paving material is often open. You can choose low-level wood decking or concrete pavers—or combine both in one multifaceted design. A blend of masonry patios and low-level decking allows great flexibility in shape, texture, and finished height. Although masonry must rest on solid ground, decks can tame sloping, bumpy, or poorly draining land.

Ready to start brainstorming? Chapter One, "A Planning Primer," will walk you through the evaluation of your present site and help you refine your thoughts. To borrow from some successful designs, take a good look at the photos in Chapter Two, "Great Patios & Decks." For shopping tips and pointers, see Chapter Three, "A Shopper's Guide."

You'll find solutions for large lots, tiny lots, and hilly lots—and many that are applicable to either wood or masonry. And since summer's always just around the corner, isn't now the time to get started?

Gently dropping from house to ground level, tiled entry landing welcomes guests.

Adding an overhead helps make aggregate patio into an outdoor dining "room."

DESIGNERS: ROGER FISKE & MARGO PARTRIDGE

A PLANNING PRIMER

Exciting as it is to fantasize about the new outdoor living space you are going to create, careful planning is what will make it become a reality.

To choose the best site, you'll need to study your property's orientation, its topography, and its weather patterns and produce a base map. This chapter will guide you.

Comparing various options in design and materials will help you visualize what you want; browse through the photos in Chapter Two, "Great Patios & Decks," for ideas. To evaluate materials, see pages 65–95.

When you've decided just what you want, this chapter will help you develop working plans. Use these to communicate with professionals (see page 21) or, if you're inclined, to build the project yourself.

Detached patio surrounds a formal garden pool. Concrete pavers are rigidly rectangular, but softened by lush border plantings. Pool provides a home for colorful water lilies; spray fountains add sound and movement.

WHAT ARE YOUR OPTIONS?

Many people regard a patio or deck as a simple rectangle off the back door. If you have a small, flat lot, maybe that's an acceptable design. But why not consider a string of patios connected by steps, or a detached "getaway" deck to make use of an attractive corner of your property? Perhaps you could even reclaim a forsaken side yard by creating a protected refuge off a bedroom or bath. Some of the possibilities are discussed below.

Basic backyard patio or deck. The standard behind-the-house rectangle doesn't have to be boring. Edgings, raised beds or benches, and maybe a gentle curve or two can give a custom look; container plants can add leafy freshness; and other amenities—perhaps a built-in hot tub or barbecue, or a decorative fountain—can tailor the space to your needs.

L- and U-shaped spaces. A house with an L or U shape almost cries out for a patio or deck. Surrounding house walls already form an enclosure; a privacy screen or a decorative overhead can formalize the design. And often such a site can be gracefully accessed from several different rooms.

Wraparounds. A flat lot is a natural candidate for a wraparound patio, which enlarges the apparent size of the house while allowing access from any room along its course. If there's a gentle grade, rise above it with a slightly elevated wraparound deck, which the Japanese call an engawa.

Detached sites. Perfect for serving as a quiet retreat, a detached patio or deck can be built on either a flat or a sloping lot and looks very much at home in a casual cottage-garden landscape. Create access to it with a direct walkway or a meandering garden path. A patio roof, privacy screen, or small fountain can make such a space even more enjoyable.

Multilevel decks and patios. A large lot, especially one with changes in elevation, can often accommodate decks and patios on different levels, linked by steps or pathways. Such a scheme works well when your outdoor space must serve many purposes.

Rooftop and balcony sites. No open space in the yard? Look up. A garage rooftop adjacent to a second-story living area might be ideal for a sunny outdoor lounging space. Or consider a small balcony patio with a built-in bench and planter box. Just be

Patio & Deck Site Options

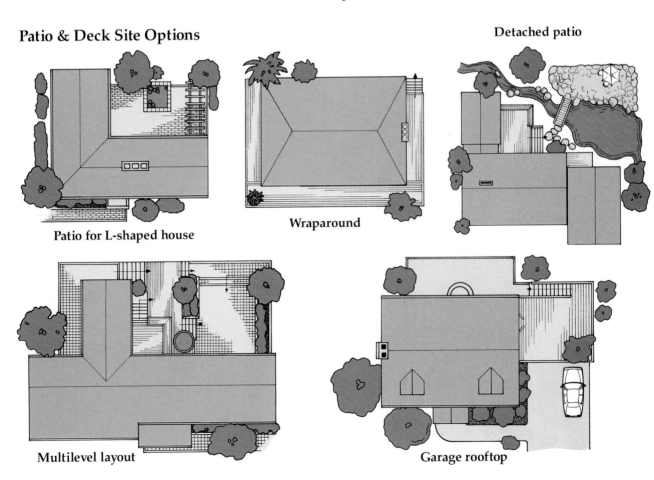

Detached patio

Patio for L-shaped house

Wraparound

Multilevel layout

Garage rooftop

sure your existing structure can take the weight of additional wood or masonry (consult an architect or structural engineer), and plan for adequate drainage.

Swimming pool surrounds. When the focus of outdoor living is a swimming pool, the setting can be formal and rectangular or more naturalistic, with the pool's form related to an informal landscape. Surround the pool with skidproof masonry and/or low-level wood decking. A dining area, a shade-creating roof, and a spa are all delightful extras.

Entry patios. Pavings, plantings, and perhaps a trickling fountain enclosed by a privacy wall can transform a boring entry path or front lawn into a private oasis. If local codes prohibit building high solid walls, try using a hedge, arbor, or trellis to let in light and air while screening off the street.

Side-yard spaces. A neglected side yard may be just the spot for a sheltered outdoor sitting area to brighten and expand a small bedroom or bathroom. And what about a sunny breakfast deck off a cramped kitchen, accessed by way of French or Dutch doors? If you're subject to fence height restrictions, use an arbor or overhead to protect privacy.

Sun-rooms. In harsh climates, the sun-room is an option as an indoor-outdoor space. Some sun-rooms can be opened up when the sun shines and battened down when hard winds blow.

Interior courtyards. If you're designing a new home, consider incorporating a private interior courtyard, or atrium. If you're remodeling, perhaps your new living space could enclose an existing patio area.

Reclaimed driveways. Your driveway can serve as a masonry "patio." Concrete turf blocks can support car traffic, but yield a softer appearance than plain asphalt; planting small spaces between pavers achieves the same effect. And enclosed by a gate and accented with complementary plantings, the semi-paved front drive becomes an entry courtyard.

Existing slabs. If you have an old slab, you can either demolish it and start over or put a new surface on top. Asphalt is best removed in most cases, but an existing concrete slab, unless heavily damaged, can serve admirably as a base for brick, pavers, tile, or stone; or you can surface it with a thin topping of colored or stamped concrete. Another possibility is to construct a low-level deck over the existing slab.

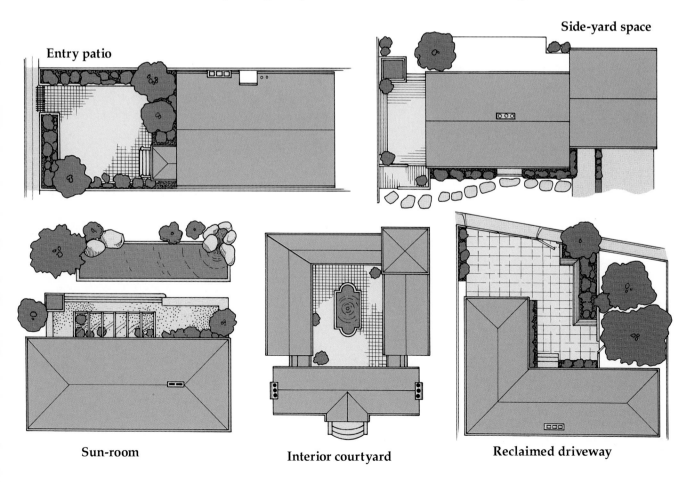

Entry patio

Side-yard space

Sun-room

Interior courtyard

Reclaimed driveway

HOW'S YOUR WEATHER?

Your site's exposure to sun, wind, rain, and snow can limit its potential as an enjoyable outdoor room. Microclimates (weather pockets created by very localized conditions) can also make a big difference. Studying these may prompt you to adjust the site of your proposed deck or patio, extend its dimensions, or change its design. You may also be able to moderate the impact of the weather with the addition of an overhead, walls, wind baffles, screens, or plantings.

Basic orientation. In general, a site that faces north is cold because it receives little sun. A south-facing patio is usually warm because it gets day-long sun. An east-facing patio is likely to be cool, receiving only morning sun. A west-facing patio can be unbearably hot because it gets the full force of the afternoon sun; in late afternoon, it may also fill with harsh glare.

Plotting the Sun's Path

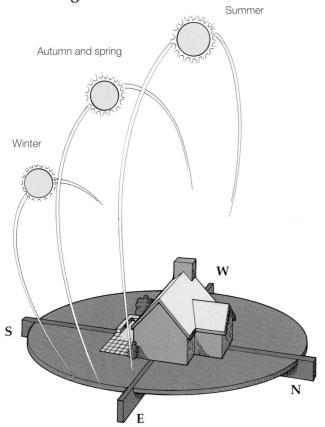

Summer

Autumn and spring

Winter

W

S

N

E

The sun's rays strike your property at predictable angles, depending on the time of year and where you live. A south-facing patio gets maximum sun and heat; a northern site is coldest.

But there are exceptions. For example, since mid-July temperatures in Phoenix often climb above 100°F, a north-facing patio there could hardly be considered "cold." In San Francisco, on the other hand, a patio with a southern or western exposure would not feel warm in July because stiff ocean breezes and chilly fogs are common then.

Seasonal paths of the sun. Another factor to consider is the sun's path during the year. As the sun passes over your house, it makes an arc that changes slightly every day, becoming higher in summer and lower in winter. Changes in the sun's path not only give us long days in summer and short ones in winter, but also alter shade patterns in your yard.

Understanding wind. Having too much wind blowing across your patio on a cool day can be just as unpleasant as having no breeze at all on a hot day. Check your lot in relation to three types of air movement: annual prevailing winds, localized seasonal breezes (daily, late-afternoon, or summer), and high-velocity blasts generated by stormy weather.

Chances are that air currents around your house are slightly different from those generally prevailing in your neighborhood. Wind flows like water—after blowing through the trees, it may spill over the house and drop onto your patio. Post small flags or ribbons where you want wind protection and note their movements during windy periods. You'll soon see where you need shelter. If you decide to build a screen or fence to block wind, remember that a solid barrier may not necessarily be the best choice. Sometimes angled baffles, lattice-type fencing, or deciduous plantings disperse wind better.

Dealing with rain or snow. If, in assessing your climate, you learn that winter storms generally blow out of the northeast, you may want to locate your patio or deck where it will take less of a beating from the weather—perhaps on the south side of the house, where it will be partially protected by trees or a roof overhang.

If you live in an area where brief summer cloudbursts frequently occur, you can extend your patio's usefulness by adding a solid roof so you can sit outdoors during warm-weather rains. It's easiest to lay the foundation for an overhead at the same time that you build the deck or patio. If you're in snow country, be sure whatever structure you plan can handle the weight of snow and ice buildup.

Microclimates

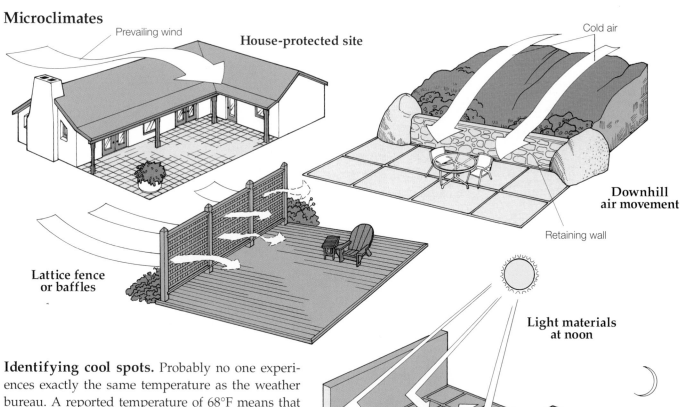

House-protected site

Prevailing wind

Cold air

Downhill air movement

Retaining wall

Lattice fence or baffles

Identifying cool spots. Probably no one experiences exactly the same temperature as the weather bureau. A reported temperature of 68°F means that a thermometer in the shade, protected from the wind, reads 68°F. If there's a 10- to 15-mile-an-hour breeze, a person in the shade will feel that the temperature is about 62°F, while someone on a sunny patio sheltered from the breeze will feel a comfortable 75° to 78°F.

Though sun and wind exposure are the major features of microclimates, they're not the only ones. Several potential microclimates are shown at right.

Remember that cold air flows downhill like water, "puddles" in basins, and can be dammed by walls or solid fences. If you build a sunken patio or one walled in by your house and a retaining wall, you may find yourself shivering at sunset while higher surroundings are quite balmy. Note any spots where cold air settles and frost is heavy.

Keep in mind, too, that certain materials reflect sun and/or heat better than others. Light-colored masonry paving and walls are great for spreading sun and heat (though they can be uncomfortably bright); and dark masonry materials retain heat longer, making evenings on the patio a little warmer. Strategically placed barrier plantings can help block wind, while allowing some breezes through. And deciduous trees can shelter a patio from hot sun in summer, yet admit welcome rays on crisp winter days, when their leaves are gone.

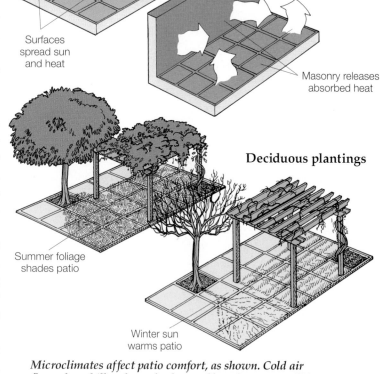

Light materials at noon

Dark materials at night

Surfaces spread sun and heat

Masonry releases absorbed heat

Deciduous plantings

Summer foliage shades patio

Winter sun warms patio

Microclimates affect patio comfort, as shown. Cold air flows downhill and may be dammed by a house or wall (at top); light-colored materials reflect light and heat, dark colors absorb it (center); deciduous plantings provide shade in summer, allow sun to penetrate in winter (at bottom).

A Sample Base Map

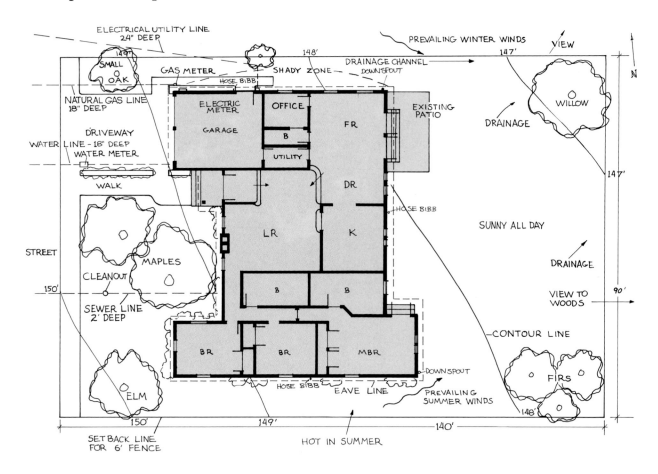

MAKING A BASE MAP

Even if you've lived with a landscape for years, mapping it can be a way to make some interesting discoveries about what you thought was familiar territory. Use your observations about your site and its setting to produce a base map like the one shown above. For pointers on choosing and using drawing tools and materials, see the facing page.

You can save yourself hours of measuring and data-gathering by obtaining dimensions, gradients, and relevant structural details from your deed map, house plans, or a contour map of your lot. If you don't have these, see if they're available at your city hall, county office, title company, bank, or mortgage company.

The information following should appear in one form or another on the base map. You'll gradually be covering a good deal of your paper with written and sketched details, so make each entry as neat and concise as possible.

■ *Boundary lines and dimensions.* Outline your property accurately and to scale, and mark its dimensions on the base map. Indicate any required setback allowances from your lot lines. Also note the relation of the street to your house.

■ *The house.* Show your house precisely and to scale within the property. Note all exterior doors (and the way each one opens), the height of all lower-story windows, and all overhangs.

■ *Exposure.* Draw a north arrow, using a compass; then note on your base map the shaded and sunlit areas of your landscape. Indicate the direction of the prevailing wind and mark any spots that are windy enough to require shielding. Also note any microclimates that you'll need to take into account.

■ *Utilities and easements.* Map the location of hose bibbs and show the locations of all underground lines, including the sewage line or septic tank. If you're contemplating a tall patio roof or elevated deck, identify any overhead lines.

If your deed map shows any easements, note them on your base map and check legal restrictions limiting development of those areas.

■ *Downspouts and drain systems.* Mark the locations of all downspouts and any drainage tiles, drainpipes, or catch basins.

■ *Gradient and drainage.* Draw contour lines on your base map, noting high and low points (here's where the official contour map is helpful). If drainage crosses boundaries, you may need to indicate the gradient of adjacent properties as well, to be sure you're not channeling runoff onto your neighbor's property.

For small, nearly level sites, you can measure slope with a level and a long straight board. More complex jobs may call for a builder's transit—and the know-how to use it.

Where does the water from paved surfaces drain? Note any point where drainage is impeded (leaving soil soggy) and any place where runoff from a steep hillside could cause erosion.

■ *Existing plantings.* If you're remodeling an old landscape, note any established plantings that you want to retain or that would require a major effort or expense to remove or replace.

■ *Views.* Note all views, attractive or unattractive, from every side of your property—the outlook will affect your enjoyment of your patio. If appropriate, you can use a ladder to check views from different elevations. Consider whether a patio, deck, or similar structure might block a favorite view from inside the house. Also take into account views into your yard from neighboring houses or streets.

CODE CONCERNS

Before you launch into the brainstorming phase, check with your local building department to find out whether you need a building permit and learn what codes affect a potential structure's design and placement. Local codes and ordinances can govern the height of an outdoor structure, its maximum coverage, the materials from which it is built, its setback from lot lines—even the nailing pattern its construction requires.

Also check your property deed for possible building easements or restrictions that might affect your project's location or design. Note any relevant code concerns on your base map.

TOOLS OF THE TRADE

To draw your base map (and, later, your final plan), you'll need 24- by 36-inch graph paper (¼-inch scale, unless the size of your property requires ⅛-inch scale), an art gum eraser, a straightedge, several pencils, and a pad of tracing paper. Optional are a drafting board, a T-square, one or more triangles, a compass, a circle template, and an architect's scale. For taking measurements in the existing landscape, choose either a 50- or a 100-foot tape measure; anything shorter is exasperating to use and can lead to inaccurate measurements.

You can draw your base map directly on graph paper or on tracing paper placed over graph paper. (If you plan to have a blueprinting company make copies of your base map, you will have to use tracing paper; a blueprint machine will not accept regular graph paper.)

And if you have access to a personal computer, don't overlook the growing collection of drawing and landscape-planning software. Unlike earlier CAD programs aimed at professionals, these newer offerings are designed for the skill levels, and limited budgets, of homeowners.

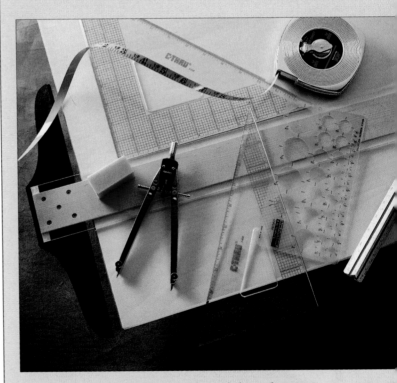

Simple drawing and measuring tools can help produce a clear, easy-to-read base map and final plan. Shown are T-square, 45° and 60° triangles, compass, circle template, eraser, architect's scale, and 50-foot tape measure.

GUIDES TO GOOD DESIGN

Regardless of the size and scope of the project, successful landscape design means suiting form to function. Architects and designers employ a number of criteria to ensure that a hardscape is useful and comfortable and that it also complements the house visually. Here are some.

■ *Meet your needs.* Your design must be able to accommodate your family's favorite activities, from relaxation and casual gatherings to children's games, barbecues, and entertaining.

■ *Suit your house.* Take time to evaluate the architectural style of your house; even if it fits no category neatly, you can probably establish its relative level of formality. A symmetrical stone or concrete patio could complement a traditional home, while a wooden deck might look best in a more naturalistic setting. Try to tie patio materials to house siding and roofing.

Also keep in scale. A large flat deck outside a small house seems out of place—more like a landing platform than an inviting outdoor living area. Likewise, a small structure off a large house feels insecure, and is seldom very useful.

■ *Protect privacy.* As an extension of your indoor living space, your patio should offer the same feeling of privacy as interior rooms do, but with no sense of confinement. Building an elevated deck, for example, can open as many unpleasant views as attractive ones—and expose you to view as well. Do you need to add screens, arbors, or landscaping to remedy the problem? Will an ivy-draped wall and a trickling fountain help buffer unwanted noise?

■ *Be aware of safety.* Patio paving materials have different properties. For example, some become slippery when wet; others are too sharp or uneven for children's games. Passage from house to patio and from deck to garden must be safe and unobstructed. Adequate lighting should be provided at steps and along garden paths.

■ *Use color.* As in a beautiful indoor room, colors should be disposed in a coordinated relationship to one another. Brick, adobe, wood, and stone have distinctive, generally earthy colors. Concrete has more industrial overtones, but can be softened with aggregate, stamping and staining, or integral color.

Even plants on or around your patio should contribute harmonious tones. Use complementary colors sparingly, as accents. Remember that all foliage is not simply "green"; the range of shades is really very large.

■ *Think transitions.* A patio or deck should entice people outdoors. So be sure to consider the transition from the inside of your house to the outside. Wide French or glass doors that open out make the outdoors look inviting and also make the interior space expand psychologically.

Try to create attractive transitions between different areas of the deck or patio and between deck and garden. The use of edgings, borders, steps, and railings can make or break your design.

■ *Attend to details.* Paying a little extra attention to the fine points of a patio or deck can add a lot to its style and substance. Improve the workmanship of the railings and trim, and the whole deck looks more intensively crafted. Nestle a built-in bench or planter into a change of level, and your patio looks gracefully tailored to the landscape.

LANDSCAPE ARCHITECT: JACK CHANDLER & ASSOCIATES

Color, texture, and detail work together in this elegant patio. Ashlar stone paving rings a garden pool, and is flanked in turn by zigzag edgings and border plantings. Flagstone knee walls help bridge garden levels. Vine-covered arbors form a green backdrop.

EXPERIMENTING WITH YOUR IDEAS

With your base map complete, you can begin trying out your ideas and determining the style of your patio. As you sketch, you'll begin to work out use areas and circulation patterns and make general decisions about what kinds of structures and amenities you'll need and where to place them.

Sketch as many designs as you can—at this stage, mistakes cost nothing. Don't limit yourself to the abstract information on the base map. Experiment directly on the landscape by pacing off areas or using stakes and strings or a garden hose to help you visualize shapes and relationships. Walk through contemplated traffic paths. Bounce your ideas off others who know the site. Then modify your sketches as needed.

Remember to think in three dimensions. This will help you balance the design elements and visualize the results so you don't confine your design to an endless horizontal plane. Slide projector planning (see page 17) can help make this process simpler.

Also try to see your design as a whole. Since a patio is related to both the garden and the house, it has an impact on both. If, for instance, you're planning a sitting area off the living room, to be shaded by an attached patio roof, you need to question whether building such an overhead might make the living room too dark. If you have young children, you should also ask yourself whether creating such a patio might eliminate the play area most easily observed from inside the house. Remember that, even with sensitive design, your project may require some trade-offs.

If your initial designs look too blocky, try cutting off some of the sharp corners, creating a polygon from a square. Or round one edge, leading the eye toward an interesting garden feature. Sometimes angling the patio or deck off the back of the house can have a dramatic effect. One of the best ways to avoid the landing-platform syndrome is to break up a large expanse into a series of smaller multilevel or satellite decks.

Defining use areas. Review how you want to use your new patio or deck. Will it be for entertaining, recreation, relaxation, storage, or some combination of these uses? Make a list and keep it before you as you draw.

A Balloon Sketch

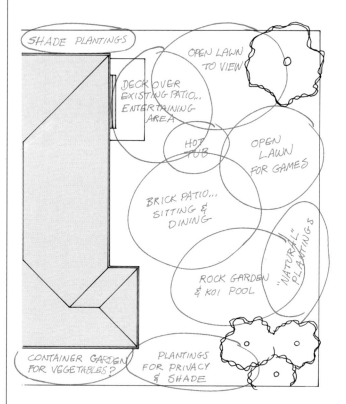

Place tracing paper over your base map; then sketch circles to indicate use areas and other features. Keep circulation patterns in mind. Consider your design as a whole, balancing design elements and relating the patio to both garden and house. Draw as many designs as you can—early mistakes cost nothing.

For each design attempt, use a separate sheet of tracing paper placed over your base map, sketching rough circles or ovals to represent the location and approximate size of each use area. For an example, see the drawing above.

As you draw, concentrate on logical placement and juxtaposition. Are you locating a children's play area in full view of your living area? Is the small, private sunning spot you envision easily accessible from the master bedroom? Do you really want a patio designed for entertaining guests to be located next to the service yard?

Examining circulation patterns. Visualize foot-traffic connections between use areas, as well as from individual areas to the house and yard. Will too much traffic be channeled through areas meant for relaxation? Can guests move easily from the entertainment area to the backyard? Can the lawn

Heights & Clearances

Clearance for table with chairs

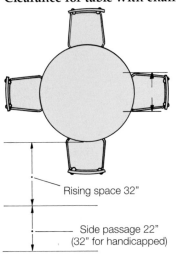

Rising space 32"

Side passage 22"
(32" for handicapped)

Pathway clearance

Service pathway

Main pathway

Bench clearance

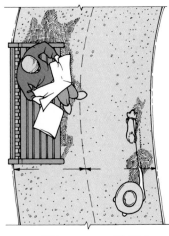

Sitting   Walking

mower or garden cart be moved from the toolshed to the lawn without disturbing someone's repose?

One way to improve access to and from the house is to add a door. But if you have to open up a wall to improve circulation, be sure you won't end up producing a traffic pattern that runs through the middle of a room.

When planning pathways, steps, and other parts of the route, you'll need to allow at least the established minimum clearances; for guidelines, see the illustrations above.

Choosing structural elements. Paving units, footpaths, raised beds, wall fountains: these and other components define the tone, texture, and ambience of your new outdoor living space. Some will work themselves very naturally into your plan; others won't fit at all. You might want to use the checklists at right to help select the features that will serve your situation best.

Observing the lay of the land. Whenever you can fit any landscape element into the existing topography with little or no disturbance of the soil, you'll save time, effort, and expense.

However, that isn't always possible. Sometimes the existing topography has inherent problems, or you realize you must alter it in order to accommodate your ideal design. Then you must grade the site—reshape it by removing soil, adding soil, or both. In most cases, it's best to consult a landscape architect or soils engineer.

If your property lies on a slope so steep that without skillful grading and terracing it would remain unstable and useless, consider constructing one or a series of retaining walls. The safest way to build the wall is to place it at the bottom of a gentle slope, if space permits, and fill in behind it. That

CHOOSING STRUCTURES

Look closely at the successful deck and patio designs shown in Chapter Two, "Great Patios & Decks." What elements do you need to include to create your own ideal outdoor environment? Which materials will work best? (Before deciding, look through the information in Chapter Three, "A Shopper's Guide.")

As you begin to firm up your design, account for the following elements:

- **Retaining walls for hilly or sloping areas**
- **Walls, fences, or screens for privacy, noise control**
- **Access from the house**
- **Decking or paving materials**
- **Steps or formal stairs for changes in level**
- **Walks and footpaths linking use areas**
- **Edgings where appropriate**

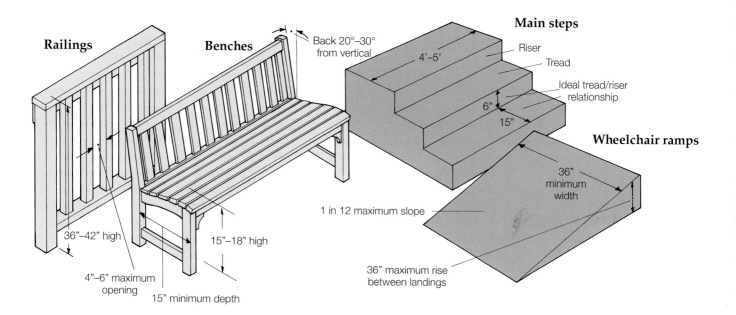

Railings

Benches

Back 20°–30° from vertical

Main steps

4'–5'

Riser

Tread

Ideal tread/riser relationship

6"

15"

Wheelchair ramps

36" minimum width

36"–42" high

4"–6" maximum opening

15" minimum depth

15"–18" high

1 in 12 maximum slope

36" maximum rise between landings

way you won't disturb the stability of the soil. Otherwise, the hill can be held either with a single high wall or with a series of low walls forming graceful terraces.

Always route water away from the house. Where property slopes toward the house, you may need to shore it up with a retaining wall, slope surfaces inward, and direct runoff to a central drain. Rapid runoff from roofs and pavement is likely to require the installation of drain tiles or catch basins.

Poor subsurface drainage can be a problem where the water table is close to the surface. Plastic drainpipes or dry wells can be the answer in many situations. But a major problem calls for a sump pump. To plan and install a drainage system for a problem hillside, get professional help.

Slide projector planning. In addition to the sketches you're making over your base map, try using a slide projector to illustrate your ideas. It's a technique landscape architects and designers employ to help clients visualize proposed designs.

Set up the projector so it focuses on the screen or wall at a level where you can work sitting down. Tape a sheet of tracing paper over the projected image of your site and begin by penciling in the proposed changes. (With features such as doors, windows, roof, and ground lines already in the slide, it should be easy for you to maintain correct scale.) Use as many sheets of paper as you need.

When you're satisfied with your design, use a dark felt-tipped pen to draw in the permanent existing background. Don't worry about capturing every detail—your eye will compensate for features that you've suggested with just a few lines.

No projector? Try enlarging photo prints of your site on a photocopier, then proceed with pencil and pen as described above.

CHOOSING AMENITIES

Although some finishing touches can be added later, now is the best time to think about the amenities you want and to sketch them on your design. Here are some items to consider:

- Patio roof or gazebo
- Garden pool, fountain, waterfall, or stream
- Spa or hot tub
- Barbecue area or kitchen facilities
- Storage cabinets or shelves
- Built-in benches or other furniture
- Outdoor lighting (120-volt or low-voltage)
- Outdoor heater or fire pit
- Hose bibb
- Raised beds for plants or built-in planters

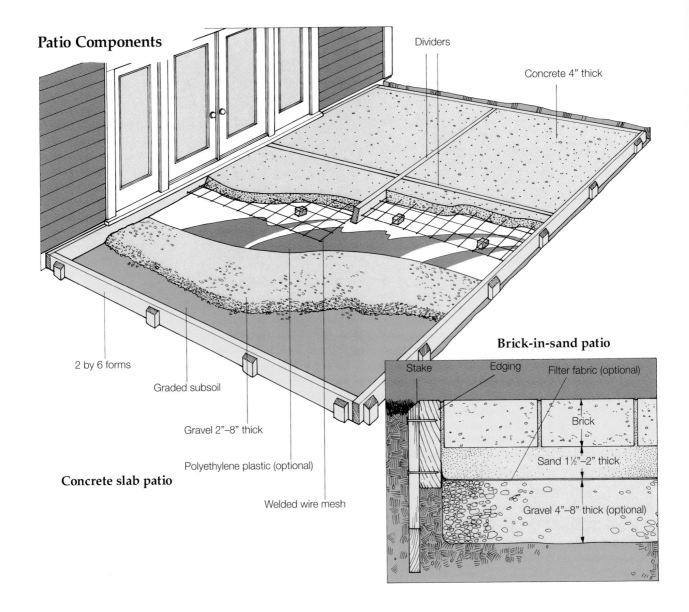

Patio Components

Dividers

Concrete 4" thick

2 by 6 forms

Graded subsoil

Gravel 2"–8" thick

Polyethylene plastic (optional)

Concrete slab patio

Welded wire mesh

Brick-in-sand patio

Stake   Edging   Filter fabric (optional)

Brick

Sand 1½"–2" thick

Gravel 4"–8" thick (optional)

PATIO PROFILES

Whether or not you intend to build your patio yourself, you'll want a basic understanding of the materials and methods involved. For starters, most patios are constructed in one of two ways—with a poured concrete slab or base or atop a bed of clean, packed sand.

A concrete slab suits heavy-use areas and formal designs. The slab should be at least 4 inches thick (see drawing above) and underlaid with 2 to 8 inches of gravel. Wire mesh helps reinforce the structure. Wooden forms define the slab's shape; they're usually removed once the concrete sets. Colored aggregates or stamped patterns can customize and soften the concrete's appearance. A thinner concrete pad, typically 3 inches thick, can serve as a base for masonry units such as ceramic tile or flagstones set in mortar (for details, see Chapter Three, "A Shopper's Guide").

A sand bed is popular for casual brick, paver, and cobblestone patios and walks, and some contractors use this method for formal work, too. A layer of gravel provides drainage and stability; damp sand is then carefully leveled—or "screeded"—on top. Paving units, either spaced or tightly butted, go atop the screeded bed, and then additional sand is cast over the surface and worked into joints to lock units in place. Edgings help define the patio and keep units from shifting.

Whatever surface you choose, you should slope it a minimum of 1 inch per 10 feet for drainage. Walkways can be angled slightly so that water is channeled away.

Deck Components

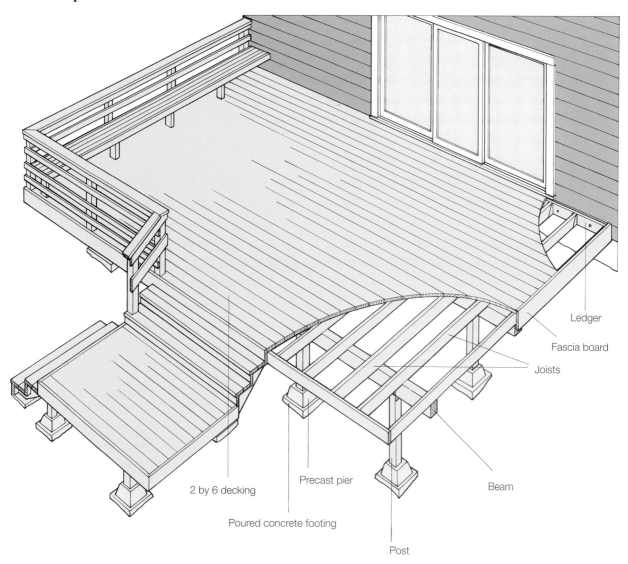

Ledger

Fascia board

Joists

2 by 6 decking

Precast pier

Poured concrete footing

Beam

Post

DECK DETAILS

If grade or drainage presents insurmountable problems, or if you simply prefer the look, feel, and "give" of a wooden surface, a deck may be the choice.

A deck can be freestanding or, as shown above, attached to the house via a horizontal ledger. Concrete footings secure precast piers or poured, tubular pads, which in turn support vertical wooden posts. One or more horizontal beams span the posts; smaller joists bridge ledger and beams. The decking itself, typically 2 by 4 or 2 by 6 lumber, is nailed or screwed to the joists. The design shown, while standard, is but one of many options.

Overheads, benches, railings, and steps are often integral to a deck's framing. While it may be feasible to add these later, it's simplest to design and build the whole project at once.

In a deck's structure, the size and spacing of each component affects the members above and below. Minimum sizes are stipulated by code. Posts taller than about 3 feet may require bracing, especially in areas prone to earthquakes or high winds. Elevated decks require railings, with slats no more than 4 to 6 inches apart (again, check local code). Fascia boards, skirts, and other trim details help dress up the basic structure.

Be sure that your decking is at least 1 inch below any door sill and that there are $\frac{1}{8}$- to $\frac{3}{16}$-inch drainage gaps between boards. Are you planning a rooftop deck? It must be sloped above an impermeable membrane—a job for a roofing contractor.

FORMALIZING YOUR PLAN

Once you've decided how you want to use your deck or patio, what types of structure will accomplish this best, and what alterations of gradient are called for, you're ready to produce your final plan. This rendering is the end result of the design process; use it for fine-tuning, for estimating materials, and when talking with professionals.

To create your plan, you'll need the same basic tools as for drawing a base map (see page 13). Most versions include a "plan" view and one or more "elevations," as shown below. (A plan view is the classic bird's-eye view of the layout; an elevation, a straight-on view, shows how the scene would look to a person standing in one spot.) Complex structures such as footings, overheads, and benches may call for additional detail drawings or cross sections.

Place a sheet of tracing paper over your base map. Label all features, as shown on the sample plan, trying to keep in mind how the plan will translate into three dimensions. Imagine color as well.

If your drawing is too cluttered to be read easily, if it calls for complicated structures, or if contractors will be relying on your plan for information, give your drawings to a design pro for a final polishing.

CAN YOU DO IT YOURSELF?

How much of the patio design and/or construction you can do yourself depends largely on the time, energy, skill, and experience you can give to the project.

If you have a knack for design, there's no reason why you can't develop a working plan, though it's wise to have at least an hour's consultation with a professional landscape architect or designer (see facing page). If you are a skilled weekend carpenter, you should have no serious problem building a simple deck or overhead. However, certain site conditions and structures may require professional help.

■ *A deck on unstable soil,* sand, mud, or water needs special foundations for support—and perhaps the advice of an engineer as well as of a builder.

■ *A deck requiring a leakproof surface* (to keep a below-deck room dry) calls for a roofing contractor.

■ *A high-level deck* or one on a steep hillside usually involves special design methods and can be too difficult for an amateur to build.

■ *Concrete work,* while straightforward, can present a logistical and physical challenge. If your job is large or complex, leave it to pros.

The Final Plan

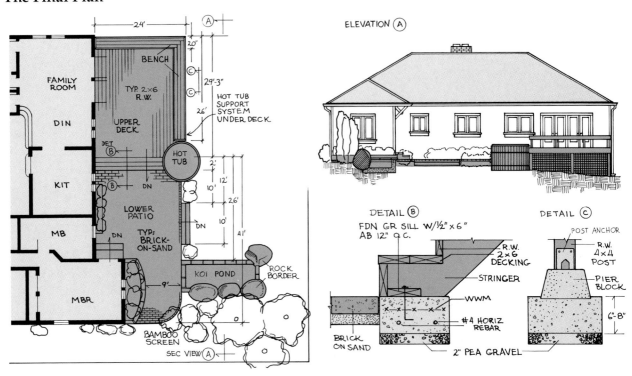

The final plan is the end result of your design work. Plan view is shown at left; an elevation (upper right) and details (lower right) complete the picture.

WORKING WITH PROFESSIONALS

Who is the right advisor to help you adapt, develop, or build your deck? Here are some of the people who can help you, along with a brief look at what they do.

Architects & Landscape Architects

These state-licensed professionals have a bachelor's or master's degree in architecture or landscape architecture. They're trained to create designs that are structurally sound, functional, and aesthetically pleasing. They also know construction materials, can negotiate bids from contractors, and can supervise the actual work. Many are willing to give a simple consultation, either in their offices or at your home, for a modest fee.

Landscape & Building Designers

Landscape designers usually have a landscape architect's education and training but not a state license. Building designers, whether licensed (by the American Institute of Building Designers) or unlicensed, may offer design help along with construction services.

Draftspersons

Drafters may be members of a skilled trade or unlicensed architects' apprentices. They can make the working drawings (from which you or your contractor can work) needed for building permits.

Structural & Soils Engineers

If you're planning to build a structure on an unstable or steep lot or where heavy wind or loads come into play, you should consult an engineer.

A soils engineer evaluates soil conditions and establishes design specifications for foundations; a structural engineer, often working with the calculations a soils engineer provides, designs foundation piers and footings to suit the site. Engineers also provide wind- and load-stress calculations as required.

General & Landscape Contractors

Licensed general and landscape contractors specialize in construction (landscape contractors specialize in garden construction), though some have design experience as well. They usually charge less for design work than landscape architects do, but their skills may be limited by a construction point of view.

Contractors may do the work themselves or assume responsibility for ordering materials, hiring qualified subcontractors, and seeing that the job is completed according to contract.

Subcontractors

If you prefer to act as your own general contractor, it's up to you to hire, coordinate, and supervise whatever subcontractors the job requires—specialists in carpentry, grading, and the like. Aside from doing the work according to your drawings, subcontractors can often supply you with product information and procure materials. Of course, you may hire other workers on your own; but in that case, you'll be responsible for permits, insurance, and payroll taxes.

LANDSCAPE ARCHITECT: JACK CHANDLER & ASSOCIATES

An elevated deck or veranda like this one is a job for the pros. Alternating strips of mahogany 2 by 2s and 2 by 4s create quiet deck accents, matched by clean, angular railing design and facings on overhead's support posts.

GREAT PATIOS & DECKS

If you're looking for inspiration, you've come to the right place. The following pages are crammed with photos that showcase both patios and decks in action. You'll find a wide range of materials; formal and informal styles; landscapes large and small; plus solutions to common—and not so common—patio problems.

As you browse, note the custom touches that turn a basic platform into a distinctive outdoor room. Pay particular attention to edgings and borders: as pros know, these transitions can make or break your design. Feel free to borrow a deck detail here, a patio accent there. Most of these ideas are appropriate for either wood or masonry, or for a mix of both.

And if it's facts and figures you're after, you'll find plenty of information on specific materials in Chapter Three, "A Shopper's Guide," beginning on page 65.

Flagstone paving frames warm evening colors in a dramatic reflecting pool, seemingly cantilevered beyond canyon rim (actually there's a retaining wall hidden from sight). Boulders form massive accents, setting off spa and waterfall. A poolside oak lives inside a circular well.

THE LOW-LEVEL DECK

Whether it's new or old, stained or sealed, wood decking at ground level feels right in almost any outdoor setting. A low-lying deck can link house and garden at flower-head height, smoothing out bumps and riding over drainage problems that might preclude masonry pavings.

LANDSCAPE ARCHITECT: KATHERINE AND STEVE EVANS   DESIGN: SARAH AND JEFF PRENTISS

Portable deck module tilts into position during installation; mods can be packed up or rearranged as whim or weather dictates. Deck supports are 2 by 6s; they radiate from 4 by 4 posts anchored to movable concrete piers.

Weathered 2 by 3s form a casual platform for relaxation or for gardening. To resist rot, place ground-level boards atop pressure-treated sleepers set in gravel.

Leisurely curves lead the eye toward the archway beyond. Low entry deck establishes a transition between house and landscape while providing a smooth surface and efficient drainage. Redwood 2 by 6 decking sits over low-profile footings and beams.

WRAPAROUNDS

A wraparound extends living space into the landscape, offering an unbeatable way to expand cramped quarters. Follow your home's shape or play off it with angular extensions or soft curves. Design a continuous boardwalk or create a series of outdoor "rooms."

LANDSCAPE DESIGNER: PETER KOENIG DESIGNS

LANDSCAPE ARCHITECT: MARY GORDON

LANDSCAPE ARCHITECT: JACK CHANDLER & ASSOCIATES

Wraparounds serve as transition zones between inside and outside. The angular deck shown above expands living space and adds visual interest to both house and garden. The patio at left moves out from the house in a graceful curve; nonslip concrete paving blends with the house's siding.

Carefully crafted brickwork links house with landscape, leads the eye—and foot—from feature to feature, and creates planting, pathway, and sitting areas. Running-bond pattern is set in sand with mortared edgings.

A cramped, steep lot presented a tough design challenge, but this multilevel, multiuse structure was a creative response. Sitting areas top retaining walls; luxurious plantings and earthy paving materials soften hard lines. Here, as with any hillscape, proper drainage is crucial.

LANDSCAPE ARCHITECT: R.M. BRADSHAW & ASSOCIATES

DESIGN: GARY MARSH/ALL DECKED OUT

Lath, wood, and metal pipe create a play of different textures in a curved, assymetrical deck cantilevered over a severe grade. To keep living-room view unobstructed, the deck steps down from a slate patio that surrounds the room.

COPING WITH SLOPES

If you're faced with a hilly, hard-to-drain site, the solution could be either a step-down, multiplatform arrangement or a cantilevered deck that can float over steep spots. Both ideas allow for exciting effects. Consider the view from inside—you may wish to drop the platform below sight.

LANDSCAPE ARCHITECT: DENNIS TROMBURG ASSOCIATES

Staggered shapes and materials create varied use zones over a slope descending from deck to aggregate patio to blue-tiled swimming pool.

AN AIR OF DETACHMENT

Getting away from it all gets tougher and tougher, but a detached patio or deck can offer restful privacy while utilizing an otherwise undeveloped garden area. Make the route to your hideaway direct or circuitous; mark the spot with an overhead or gazebo, or use subtle screening.

LANDSCAPE ARCHITECT: EMERY ROGERS AND ASSOCIATES

Set in a redwood grove, a large detached deck continues the grade of uphill areas. Cantilevered sections gain airy views and dramatic lift while allowing water and oxygen to reach trees' root systems. Rocks bordering the spa double as steps.

This detached patio makes a quiet spot for flower-surrounded lounging. A tiny paved clearing, borrowed from the garden, contains just enough solid brick to anchor chairs, drinks, and a thick novel or two.

DESIGN: MICHAEL SHULTZ

Mortared flagstone pad is edged with both natural coastal plants and domesticated landscaping; a pocket in the paving invites the greenery in.

31

A small rear-garden hardscape integrates patio and plantings with a central fountain. Paving is rock-salt concrete accented with bands of stone tiles. The decorative pool below the soothing-sounding waterfall can be heated for a relaxing soak.

DESIGN: CHRIS JACOBSON

This lot is just 24 feet wide, but making the most of it. Third-floor view shows multiple decks occupying most of the garden, with planting pockets along outer edges. Simple trellis structures topped by 4 by 4s support vines that shade seating below.

SMALL-SPACE STRATEGIES

When space is lacking, your landscape must work harder. Vertical stacking is one way to handle sloped or multistory layouts. Or intensify your space by creating small multipurpose areas. To protect privacy, use tall plants; to mask noise, try a trickling fountain.

LANDSCAPE ARCHITECT: RANSOHOFF, BLANCHFIELD & JONES, INC.

Light shaft reaches down to first-floor pocket patio, bringing garden life to a potentially neglected spot. All paving sections are movable, and drainage below was carefully planned. A simple basin fountain adds the murmur of moving water.

LANDSCAPE ARCHITECT: LOUIS J. MARANO

Aggregate side-yard patio, tucked off the kitchen, guards its privacy with brick walls that echo the house construction. Brick edgings and border plantings soften the look.

UP-FRONT IDEAS

Though we tend to picture the "patio area" as being behind the house, why not look out front? An entry patio stretches usable space and welcomes guests, too. Soften a driveway with turf blocks or planting pockets. An arbor, trellis, or glass-block wall lends privacy while letting light in.

Lowered courtyard patio of precast concrete pavers sits between house and garage, enclosed by a retaining wall, steps, and an angled deck. Tall wall helps screen the garden from a nearby street.

Serpentine bands of stone and plants ease the edges of a concrete driveway. The shape and slope of the lot require the driveway to double as main house access, but now there's an attractive meander toward the entry. Pockets of flowering thyme lend color and textural contrast.

Build a front-yard hardscape from either wood or masonry. Below left, stained cedar deck offers broad landings for easy access; subtle changes of angle break up the approach visually. Below right, what appear to be flagstones on steroids are actually irregularly shaped pads of stained concrete. With limited space in the backyard, owners wanted a driveway that could also serve as a play area and patio.

Enclosed patios form an effective bridge between indoor and outdoor living spaces. In the dramatic design below, a craggy peak creates a majestic backdrop for a "furnished" outdoor room. In the sheltered sitting area at right, a wide arch opens toward a soothing spa.

INSIDE OUT

In temperate climates, you can relax the line between indoors and outdoors, creating a leisurely transition between the two. Add French doors, a window wall, or bifold doors. And don't rule out the classic porch, currently enjoying a deserved comeback.

DESIGNER: ROBERT CURRIE

A shaded porch between the house and garden is a tranquil spot for an old-fashioned swing. In place of the more usual raised decking are rustic stone slabs.

POOL PLATFORMS

Today's pool can do more than accommodate swimmers. It can also serve as a reflecting pond, a fountain, a spa. The surround sets the mood. Nonslip masonry is safest, but wood stays cooler underfoot. Edgings can lend a starkly geometric pool more informal, easygoing lines.

ARCHITECT: CHURCHILL & HAMBELTON ARCHITECTS

Naturalistic pool, bounded by imposing boulders, reflects sunrise in its still surface. Garden walls built from smooth river rocks echo the motif.

LANDSCAPE DESIGNER: PETER KOENIG DESIGNS

"Classic" is the concept here, as Saltillo pavers, formal columns, and concrete edgings frame a blue, blue pool. Poolside views open toward rolling countryside with stately oaks.

LANDSCAPE ARCHITECT: ROYSTON, HANAMOTO, ALLEY & ABEY

A step-up deck next to the pool houses a spa and provides a stage for entertaining or sunbathing. Railing of pipe and solid wood allows view, yet offers a sense of enclosure.

SPAS & HOT TUBS

Spas come in many materials, from streamlined acrylic to homey wood to formal concrete. Place your spa poolside or sequester it in a private nook. Whether futuristic or naturalistic, your spa can also serve as a garden pool or fountain. Be sure to plan shelter from wind, rain, and the neighbors.

An octagonal spa, framed by brick surround with bench seating, is the centerpoint of a garden gazebo structure. Fountain's waterfall fills the spa. Gazebo's central roof opening allows starry views on clear evenings.

LANDSCAPE ARCHITECT: RANSOHOFF, BLANCHFIELD & JONES, INC.

Tucked into alcoves, the tubs and spa on the facing page look great and offer great privacy. The 5-foot-diameter hot tub at top left nestles into an edge of the deck; tiers of curved steps can be used for seating. Concrete steps lead down to the rectangular spa at top right, bordered by handsome grasses. In the covered patio at left, hot tub platform fits into a protected corner.

UP ON THE ROOF

In the quest for space, don't rule out a rooftop aerie. It could be a perch adjacent to the living room, kitchen, or master bedroom suite—perhaps on the roof of the garage. Erect a wind screen, add a hose bibb, grow container plants, and train a vine along a trellis.

LANDSCAPE ARCHITECT: ROYSTON, HANAMOTO, ALLEY & ABEY

A parking deck perches over a workout studio on a steep hillside lot; the overhang contributes extra room. Like nearly all cantilevered decks, this one was designed by qualified professionals.

LANDSCAPE ARCHITECT: MANUELA ANNE KING/MARCIA VALLIER

While not all rooftop views are this inspiring, you might look up to find a new vantage point as well as usable outdoor space. This patio combines 2 by 6 decking with "faux" limestone tiles (actually painted, textured concrete).

If urban congestion gets you down, look up. This rooftop layout unites wooden decking, planter boxes, and a greenhouse unit as one compact, trellis-topped oasis.

LANDSCAPE ARCHITECT: RANSOHOFF, BLANCHFIELD & JONES, INC.
LANDSCAPE CONTRACTOR: LEHMAN LANDSCAPING CO.

This design takes advantage of a change in garden level. A structural extension of the upper garden becomes the poolhouse roof—and a sunny veranda overlooking the pool. Brickwork ties the levels together.

Steps not only direct traffic, they also provide a canvas for varied accents and details. Copper step light (left) looks great, aids safe footing at night. At center, alternating butt joints form strong wood diagonal. Railroad ties (right), dyed dark blue, make sturdy risers and hold mortared brick in check.

LANDSCAPE ARCHITECT: JACK CHANDLER & ASSOCIATES   LANDSCAPE ARCHITECT: JOHN HERBST JR. & ASSOCIATES

LANDSCAPE ARCHITECT: ROBERT W. CHITTOCK & ASSOCIATES

How do you integrate a flight of aggregate stairs into the garden? Widen them to form a landing. Then soften them with ground covers and border plantings. The result is a graceful set of landscaped terraces.

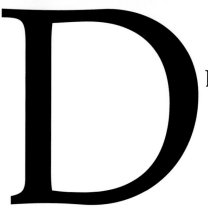

DECISIVE STEPS

Garden steps shuttle traffic. They can also offer design opportunities. Think of them as transition zones between levels; extensions might double as benches, planters, or display perches. Be sure the dimensions are comfortable—not too long, and not too steep.

LANDSCAPE ARCHITECT: DELANEY & COCHRAN

Purple pavers are the treads, blue-tinted concrete the risers along this colorful entry walk. Note how colors are repeated in front door and house trim.

RAILINGS & OTHER DETAILING

Any deck or patio dropoff of more than 30 inches requires a railing or similar barrier. Beyond safety, railings contribute an important design element, too. What's the view? Use railings to frame it or block it. Fill gaps with vertical slats, safety glass, or screening.

DESIGN: SEAN HOPPER

DESIGN: ROBERT HAUCK/MR. DECK

Railings customize a deck and create a safe restraint—or at least mark edges. Child-safe netting at upper left snaps into place, can be removed for view or when entertaining. Waterside railing at upper right, suitable for adults only, incorporates hawser-size rope, truck running lights, and "pilings." Routed grooves and metal horse-tie loops secure the rope.

LANDSCAPE ARCHITECT: JAMES BRADANINI, BRADANINI & ASSOCIATES

Wrought iron provides the framework and heavy safety glass fills the gaps while maintaining views. Railing repeats around lower porch and along steps.

DESIGN: JOHN CAMPBELL/METALURGE

The railing above started with an outline "drawing" of solid metal rods that were heated, bent, and welded to form shapes echoing the contours of distant hills. Cutouts of expanded metal lath (used in stucco work) have been welded to the rod.

Custom baked-enamel steel railings, available in many colors, combine with steel cable and turnbuckles for a clean, uncluttered look. Though materials are industrial, the style looks appropriate with just about any deck.

Classic wood design combines bolt-on 4 by 4 posts with doubled 2 by 6 rails. Verticals are stock redwood 2 by 2s. An electric router helps round lumber edges for a more finished look.

ARCHITECT: MARK MERYASH, AIA

LANDSCAPE ARCHITECT: JOHN HERBST JR. & ASSOCIATES

SITTING PRETTY

Architectural built-ins supplement portable patio furniture and free floor space for other uses. Build benches into wide steps or transitions between levels. Make them from nonslip masonry, wood, or metal; and be sure to plan for drainage. For fun, add a nook for a porch swing or hammock.

DESIGN: GARY MARSH/ALL DECKED OUT

Set beside an ancient oak, this curving redwood deck is a place to enjoy the woodsy outdoors. Built-in seating follows the curves; handsomely crafted railings lend the feeling of quality furniture.

DESIGN: ROBERT HAUCK/MR.DECK

Novel seating creates dynamic deck accents, too. Above, seating platforms step down beside stairs forming break in upper deck's benches. Right, triangular built-in bench follows the line of a contoured, cantilevered deck alcove.

A simple but graceful patio planter bed doubles as a bench; stuccoed knee wall is capped with bent wood. The cactus garden helps keep patio loungers alert.

ARCHITECT: MORIMOTO ARCHITECTS

An overhead can provide solid shelter or simply celebrate space. The house-attached overhead at left teams with knee walls and sandstone paving to form a protected outdoor room or ramada. The column-supported structure below marks a detached garden patio rimmed by lily- and dahlia-dabbled terraces.

LANDSCAPE ARCHITECT: R.M. BRADSHAW & ASSOCIATES
LANDSCAPE CONTRACTOR: FISKE LANDSCAPING

OVERHEAD OPTIONS

Overheads may be house-attached or freestanding, sleek or woodsy, dramatic or understated. One can give you heavy shade or form just the suggestion of an arbor. If you wish, surround the protected area with knee walls or privacy screens, and train plants up and over the top.

LANDSCAPE ARCHITECT: JACK CHANDLER & ASSOCIATES
DESIGN: KELLY PACIFIC CONSTRUCTION CO.

DESIGN: BLUE SKY DESIGNS INC., HALF MOON BAY

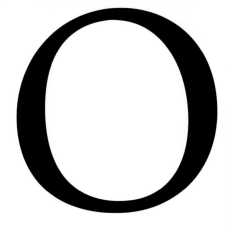

Like Victorian gingerbread, this lattice-intensive patio structure combines intricate angles and curves to create feeling of light and grace.

Open steel gridwork, supported by angular stuccoed columns, roofs a long patio promenade. Metal styling amplifies the house's clean lines, also allows long spans between columns.

GAZEBOS

Gazebos are being rediscovered. Evocative of country bandstands on summer evenings, they become poetic-looking retreats and romantic garden destinations. They take beautifully to amenities: decorative path lights or downlights, built-in benches or swings, fountains or spas.

Rising as gracefully as the conifers nearby, skylight-capped gazebo shelters a poolside dining area. Trim is mahogany; rails are steel. Flagstone paving makes clean, solid flooring with a natural look.

Open-sided gazebo perches at garden's edge, creating a focal point for a relatively formal landscape. The weather vane gives a nod to the rural past.

LANDSCAPE ARCHITECT: JACK CHANDLER & ASSOCIATES
GAZEBO DESIGN: DON BRANDENBURGER

LANDSCAPE ARCHITECT: R.M. BRADSHAW & ASSOCIATES

A storybook vision from an upstairs window, this detached gazebo accents a garden rich in both drama and intimacy. Slate quad marks the path, giving way to elegantly crafted redwood bridge and structure.

LANDSCAPE ARCHITECT: R.M. BRADSHAW & ASSOCIATES

Patio storage needs can provoke awkward design, but this recycling shed is a good-looking solution. Slatted doors provide ventilation—as do openings in "birdhouse" cupola. Elevated curb aids drainage, allows easy cleanup.

DESIGN: DECKDESIGN

Built-in bench seat lifts on stout hinges to reveal ample storage space inside. Bench is constructed with redwood 4 by 4 posts and 2 by 4 and 2 by 6 framing; cleats hold surface 2 by 6s steady.

STORAGE SOLUTIONS

How do you stash away all those outdoor accessories when you don't need them, yet keep them nearby for when you do? Open space below a deck's substructure can be enclosed to make storage cabinets. Or add decktop benches with hinged lids. The age-old garden shed is another option.

LANDSCAPE ARCHITECT: JOHN HERBST, JR.

DESIGN: BOB WATERMAN

Deck owners have a love-hate relationship with hoses. To keep the hose handy but hidden, this designer built a storage box (equipped with faucet) between joists. The recess is topped with a hatch to match 2 by 6 decking.

Area below raised deck yielded a head-height closet for outdoor gear and pool equipment. For weathertight storage, the surface above must be sealed.

THE OUTDOOR KITCHEN

Rotisserie, smoker, wok, or deep fryer: open-air cooking has evolved from simple barbecue to full-fledged outdoor kitchen. The cooking area should be convenient to the house (consider a pass-through). Don't forget some way to batten down hatches in the off-season.

ARCHITECT: J. ALLEN SAYLES

Outdoor kitchen built into a protected alcove contains barbecue, vent hood, sink, and plenty of storage cabinetry. In winter, bifold doors seal off the area.

Patio niche accommodates a commercial gas barbecue as well as electrical outlets, downlights, and a built-in fan. Detailing includes handsome brick and tile.

A weatherproof griddle, two gas barbecues, a pair of gas burners, and ample storage equip this outdoor cooking area. The tiled counter is just the right height for seated diners.

DESIGN: JO ANN MESSING/FORTNER MILLWORK

LANDSCAPE ARCHITECT: THOMAS L. BERGER

An oven fits in a separate chimney between the large, patio-warming fireplace on the left and the smaller one on the right. Gas jet regulates the oven to allow brined salmon to smoke slowly at low heat and duck or Chinese-style pork to roast at higher temperatures.

LANDSCAPE ARCHITECT: RICHARD WILLIAM WOGISCH

Is your look formal or informal? Below, classic masonry beds suit the formal style of the house. But at right, corrugated steel culvert pipes are inset through deck cutouts to form more eccentric planters. Bottomless, they drain to soil below.

PLANTERS & POCKETS

Built-in planting spaces give a custom touch to your landscape. Add formal masonry beds or leave planting pockets between paving units (run drip tubing below the surface). Incorporate planters into steps or level changes. Sculpt cutouts for tree wells to bring life to wooden decks.

DESIGN: JUANITA DICKSON

LANDSCAPE ARCHITECT: MARY GORDON

An elevated deck's zigzag railings are sandwiched in color. Container plants sit on deck's surface and hanging planters are suspended outside.

Morning sun casts tulip shadows across tightly fitted flagstone paving. The elliptic shape of this planting pocket gives it an informal, unpredictable quality.

Plants grow in the ground, up the walls, and overhead, obliterating hard-edge boundaries in the patio below. The sundial, the inviting wooden chair, and occasional container plants add to the romantic character. The adobe patio at left also merges paving with garden, as plants spill forth from open spaces beside edging of broken concrete.

GARDEN MEETS PATIO

A cottage garden blurs the edge between patio and borders, stretches planting space, and softens paving or low-level decking. Let edgings merge into plantings, or mark the transition zone with planting pockets or containers. A trellis or arbor can gain you additional growing space overhead.

DESIGN: LEW WHITNEY / ROGERS GARDENS

LANDSCAPE CONTRACTOR: ROB LANE

The contrast between brick and flagstone provides color and textural interest, while pockets of gray-green plantings tie the composition together. The plants, which range from ground-hugging woolly thyme to spiky fox red curly sedge, are eye-attracting accents.

A SPLASH OF WATER

Whether trickling as a wall fountain, meandering as a stream, or collected as a full-scale garden pool complete with lilies and fish, water brings magic and repose to the patio picture. Your water feature may be formal or informal, edged with angular brick or rimmed with native boulders.

Water makes this narrow urban yard into a small oasis. The waterfall masks sound, and aggregate stepping stones involve inhabitants with the landscape. A pool pump collects water and sends it back to the top, where it's used again and again.

Today's spas can also serve as garden pools and fountains. In this case, three decorative water outlets fill a spa; complementary tile colors link the fountain to the spa and its surround.

LANDSCAPE ARCHITECT: RANSOHOFF, BLANCHFIELD & JONES, INC.

LANDSCAPE DESIGNER: MARK GENNARO/LANDSHAPE, INC.

A plant-filled pond turns this owner-built deck into a riparian retreat just a few feet from the house. Rounded ends give a water-smoothed look to 2 by 6 redwood decking. The pond's shell was formed with chicken wire, steel reinforcing rods, and heavy wire mesh, then two layers of concrete.

A SHOPPER'S GUIDE

Whether you are leaning toward wood or masonry, this chapter can help you sort out your options. Here we focus on the materials that build your new outdoor recreation space. We'll try to demystify some of the ritual and jargon surrounding lumberyards and garden centers. Special features along the way help you decipher the intricacies of garden-pool hardware, adobe construction, and outdoor lighting systems.

Local knowledge can be a big help. Ask your building department or garden supplier about the best deck stain, tile type, or base treatment for use in your area. Be sure to check current local stock before buying; new products appear constantly.

If you're building the project yourself, you may wish to consult the *Sunset* titles *Decks* and *The Complete Patio Book* for detailed help with construction.

As shown in this collection, masonry units come in a wide assortment of shapes, colors, and textures. Uniform bricks and concrete pavers, grouped at far left, give way to rougher stone cobbles at center. At right, rounded river rocks sit atop a stack of formal tiles, both ceramic and stone. A hand-painted accent tile holds down the foreground.

LUMBERYARD PRIMER

A wooden deck—either freestanding or house-attached—provides a solid, relatively durable surface requiring little or no grading and a minimum of maintenance. Because decking is raised above the ground and can dry quickly, it will survive longer under adverse conditions than other wooden systems.

Basic deck components are shown on page 19.

Wood rounds, blocks, and timbers are user-friendly materials that allow the builder a good deal of creative freedom. But don't expect them to last like decking, especially in damp or humid climates.

Lumber Terms

The lumber you use strongly influences your deck's appearance and takes the largest bite out of your project dollar, so it pays to learn the basics of lumber types and terminology before you make final plans.

Softwood and hardwood. All woods are one or the other. The terms don't refer to a wood's relative hardness, but to the kind of tree from which it comes. Softwoods come from evergreens (conifers), hardwoods from broadleafed (deciduous) trees. Because hardwoods are generally costlier and more difficult to work with, they've not often been used for deck construction. However, more economical offerings of hardwoods such as mahogany, ipe (a South American newcomer), and teak (the boat builder's favorite) have recently been introduced to the market.

Heartwood, sapwood, and grain. A wood's properties are determined by the part of the tree it came from. The inactive wood nearest the center of a living tree is called heartwood. Sapwood, next to the bark, contains the growth cells. Heartwood is more resistant to decay; sapwood is more porous and absorbs preservatives and other chemicals more efficiently.

Depending on the cut of the millsaw, lumber will have parallel grain lines running the length of the board (vertical grain), a marbled appearance (flat grain), or a combination of the two. Vertical-grain lumber is less likely to cup and generally looks better, but it often costs more.

Close-up on Lumber

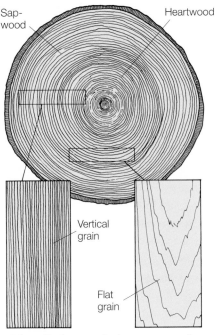

Sapwood

Heartwood

Vertical grain

Flat grain

A board's characteristics vary according to how it's cut from the log.

Redwood grades range from clear (far left) to rough and knotty (center). Pressure-treated timbers and railroad ties (right) make great edgings.

Multilevel deck glows with warm sunset light. Decking boards are clear redwood 2 by 6s. Built-in benches, wide steps, and matching railings add finishing touches. Note how deck cutouts house mature oak trees.

Elevated redwood deck hovers over coastal hills. Its rustic look and feel are due to knotty decking that's pressure-washed annually. Spaces between railings are filled with fence wire, repeating country theme and preserving open views.

Among heartwoods, the most decay-resistant and termite-proof species are cypress, redwood, and cedar. This resistance, combined with their natural beauty, makes them a favorite for decking. On the other hand, they tend to be softer, weaker, and more expensive than ordinary structural woods such as Douglas fir and Western larch. To get the best of both worlds, most professional designers favor Douglas fir and the other structural woods for a deck's substructure, but opt for decking, benches, and railings of redwood or cedar. For any wood nearer than 6 inches to the ground or to concrete foundations, though, choose decay-resistant heartwood or pressure-treated wood (see page 69).

Grades. Lumber is sorted and graded at the mill. Generally, lumber grades depend on several factors: natural growth characteristics (such as knots), defects resulting from milling errors, and commercial drying and preserving techniques that affect each piece's strength, durability, and appearance.

A stamp on lumber may identify its quality, moisture content, grade name, and (often) species and a grading agency (such as WWP for Western Wood Products Association). In most cases, the fewer the knots and other defects, the costlier a board or length of dimension lumber.

Rough and surfaced lumber. Nearly all lumberyards handle both rough and surfaced lumber. Rough

Low-level cedar deck floats above rock garden and bridges garden pool; 2 by 3 decking boards are finished with semitransparent stain.

LANDSCAPE ARCHITECT: LANKFORD ASSOCIATES

lumber tends to be available only in lower grades, with a correspondingly greater number of defects and a higher moisture content. Surfaced lumber, the standard for most construction and a must for formal decking, comes in nearly all grades.

Nominal and surfaced sizes. Be aware that a finished "2 by 4" is not 2 inches by 4 inches. The nominal size of lumber is designated before the piece is dried and surfaced; the finished size is smaller. Here are some examples:

2 by 3 = 1½" by 2½"
2 by 4 = 1½" by 3½"
2 by 6 = 1½" by 5½"
4 by 4 = 3½" by 3½"

Treated Lumber

Though redwood, cedar, and cypress heartwoods resist decay and termites, other woods that contact the ground or trap water will rot and lose their strength. For this reason, less durable types such as Southern pine and Western hem-fir are often factory-treated with preservatives that guard against rot, insects, and other sources of decay. These woods are generally less expensive and in many areas more readily available than redwood, cedar, and cypress. They can be used for surface decking as well as for structural members such as posts, beams, and joists.

Working with treated lumber isn't always a pleasure. Unlike redwood and cedar, which are easy to cut and nail or screw, treated wood is often hard and brittle and is more likely to warp or twist. Moreover, some people object to its typically greenish-brown color (though applying a semitransparent stain can conceal it) and the staplelike treatment incisions that usually cover it (some types come without these marks).

Because the primary preservative used contains chromium, a toxic metal, you should wear safety goggles and breathing protection when cutting treated lumber, and you should never burn it.

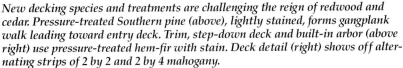

New decking species and treatments are challenging the reign of redwood and cedar. Pressure-treated Southern pine (above), lightly stained, forms gangplank walk leading toward entry deck. Trim, step-down deck and built-in arbor (above right) use pressure-treated hem-fir with stain. Deck detail (right) shows off alternating strips of 2 by 2 and 2 by 4 mahogany.

A SHOPPER'S GUIDE **69**

Deck Fasteners & Hardware

Nails, screws, and metal framing connectors are essential to building—without them, a deck would be nothing but a stack of lumber. Here's a look at the kinds of hardware you'll probably need.

Nails. Hot-dipped galvanized box or common nails are used for most outdoor deck construction. Nails are sold in boxes (weighing 1, 5, or 50 pounds) or loose in bins. A nail's length is indicated by a "penny" designation ("penny" is abbreviated as "d," from the Latin *denarius*). The equivalents in inches for the most common nails are as follows:

4d = 1½"	6d = 2"	8d = 2½"
10d = 3"	16d = 3½"	20d = 4"

Most decking jobs are done with 8d and 16d nails. Buy hot-dipped galvanized, aluminum, or stainless steel nails; other types will rust. In fact, even the best hot-dipped nail will rust in time, particularly at the exposed head, where its coating has been battered by a hammer.

Deck screws. Though they're more expensive than nails, coated or galvanized deck screws provide secure, high-quality fastening. Screws have several advantages over nails: they don't pop up as readily, their coating is less likely to be damaged during installation, and their use eliminates the problem of hammer dents in the decking. You'll find them surprisingly easy to drive in soft woods such as redwood and cedar if you use an electric drill or screw gun with an adjustable clutch and a Phillips screwdriver tip.

Choices in deck fasteners include galvanized box nails (bottom), deck screws (center), and deck clips (top right). Framing connectors (top left) help join structural components.

Choose screws that are long enough to penetrate joists at least as deep as the decking is thick (for 2 by 4 or 2 by 6 decking, buy 3-inch screws). Screws are sold by the pound or, at a substantial savings, in 25-pound boxes.

Deck clips. To eliminate visible fasteners, you can use special deck-fastening clips. Nailed to the sides of decking lumber and secured to joists, these fasteners hide between deck boards. Deck clips also elevate boards a hair off the joist, discouraging the rot that wood-to-wood contact may breed. On the down side, clips are more expensive to buy and more time-consuming to install than nails or screws.

Framing connectors. The photo on the facing page shows the most commonly used framing connectors, including joist hangers, post anchors, and post caps. Galvanized metal connectors can help prevent lumber splits commonly caused by toenailing two boards together. They are easy to use and they strengthen joints. When using framing connectors, be sure to buy the sizes and types of nails specified by the manufacturer.

In main structural connections, use bolts or lag screws. To join a ledger to a masonry wall, use expanding anchor bolts.

Deck Finishes

There's no substitute for using decay-resistant wood like heart redwood or pressure-treated lumber where deck members come in contact with soil or are embedded in concrete. Applying a water repellent, a semitransparent stain, or a solid-color stain can, however, protect other parts of a deck and preserve its beauty.

Finishes change a wood's color or tone and may mask its grain and texture. Whatever product you choose, it's best to try it on a sample board before getting your entire deck committed to it. Always read labels: some

products should not be applied over new wood; others may require a sealer first.

Water repellent. Also known as water sealers, these products protect decking wood. Clear sealers won't color wood, but they darken it slightly. These products allow the wood to gradually fade to a neutral gray. You can buy them in either oil- or water-base versions. Many formulations include both UV-blockers and mildewcides. Some brands come in slightly tinted, dye-color versions.

Don't use clear surface finishes such as spar varnish or polyurethane on decks. They wear quickly and are very hard to renew. They're also expensive.

Semitransparent stains. These contain enough pigment to tint the wood's surface but not enough to mask the natural grain completely. You can find both water- and oil-base versions. Usually one coat is sufficient. Besides traditional grays and wood tones, you'll find products for "reviving" a deck's color or for dressing up pressure-treated wood.

Solid-color stains. These include both solid-color deck stains and deck paint. Solid-color stains are essentially paints; their heavy pigments cover wood grain completely. You can usually get any available paint color mixed into this base. Even though these products are formulated for foot traffic, you'll probably have to renew them frequently.

If you do go this route, don't choose stains or paints intended for house siding; they won't last.

Deck finishes offer plentiful choices in color and protection. Shown at right, from top to bottom: unfinished redwood board; clear water sealer; tinted oil-base repellent; semitransparent gray stain; and red solid-color stain.

BRICK

A rich palette of colors and a broad range of styles make brick a top choice for garden paving. With the dozens of kinds available, it gives you more options than any other paving material.

Brick Types

Brick's use dates back at least 6,000 years. To make bricks, clay is first mixed with water, then machine-extruded or hand-molded into traditional forms, then fired in a kiln. The color is a result of the clay's chemical composition and the way it's fired.

In addition to the familiar orange-red, some manufacturers offer bricks in colors created by the addition of minerals to the clay. Manganese can give a metallic blue tone. Iron pro-

Formal red-brick paving sports solid, mortared joints. Basket-weave pattern is set off by precise white grout lines.

Brick samples range from machine-extruded common type (far left) to brand-new "used" bricks to hand-molded ones (far

duces a dark speckling. "Flashed" brick is fired unevenly to darken either its face (large surface) or edge.

Used brick has uneven surfaces and streaks of old mortar that can look very attractive in an informal pavement. Manufactured used or "rustic" bricks cost about the same as the genuine article and are easier to find. Low-density firebricks, blond-colored and porous, provide interesting accents but don't wear well as general paving.

Brick dimensions vary according to the manufacturer. For one company, a standard size might be 2¼ by 3⅝ by 7⅝ inches. For another, it may be 2½ by 3⅞ by 8¼.

Other sizes include split (half as thick as standard brick); thin (⅜ to ½ inch thick), also called veneer, which must be applied on a concrete base and set in mortar; and Norman (about 11½ inches long).

Depending on how the bricks were made, surface texture may be rough or smooth (the smoothest ones may be too slippery for paving). Hand-molded bricks have a rough texture and slightly irregular shapes.

Railroad ties restrain a charming brick-in-sand patio, also set in basket weave. Soil-filled joints support growth of soft-looking moss.

right). Color comes from chemical composition of clay and firing method and temperature.

Deciding on a Design

Countless patterns can be created when designing with brick, and each one elicits a different reaction. Six of the most popular are shown below right. If you want to unify an area, use a single pattern. Introduce a new pattern to signal a transition from one area of the garden to another. If you decide to mix several kinds of brick in a pattern, make sure the sizes of all the bricks are exactly the same. When using mortar (see below), you must account for the mortar joints.

Sand or Mortar?

Brick set in sand or rock fines (a mix of grain sizes) is casual-looking and less uniform, with more textural variation. (For a construction detail, see page 18.) This method allows percolation, which is important when installing a patio over tree roots. Bricks in sand can move around and may have to be reset, but repairs are easier than with grouted bricks.

When set in mortar and grouted, brick has cleaner lines, which can give a design a more formal or contemporary look. The surface is easier to clean and better for walking in high heels (if joints are wider than ¼ inch).

The grout is a very important part of the overall design. Browns soften or blend with the design, whereas lighter colors like blues, greens, and grays may emphasize it.

Shopping for Brick

You can find bricks at masonry suppliers or building and landscape supply yards; look in the Yellow Pages of your telephone directory under "Brick" or "Building Materials." Bricks cost upwards of 25 cents each.

You may want to shop around, since suppliers in the same region may stock different types of brick.

Curved design using five kinds of brick gives this small patio strong character; each unit was hand-cut to fit.

Six Brick Patterns

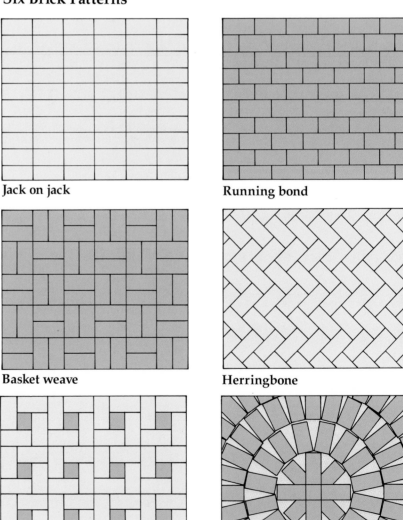

Jack on jack

Running bond

Basket weave

Herringbone

Pinwheel

Whorled

A GUIDE TO GARDEN POOLS

You may be surprised to learn how easy it can be to bring the soothing sound and sight of water to your patio environment. Pool materials range from naturalistic liners through formal concrete to a new generation of pumps, filters, and accessories. Here's a brief look at the choices. For further details, see the *Sunset* book *Garden Pools, Fountains & Waterfalls*.

Pool Materials

Flexible liners are the big news in garden pools, and you'll find some type of liner in virtually every mail-order garden-pool catalog. These stout sheets—20 to 30 mils and thicker—are designed especially for garden pools. Though PVC plastic is the standard material, it becomes brittle with exposure to the sun's rays and only lasts about 10 years. More UV-resistant—but twice the price—are industrial-grade PVC and butyl-rubber liners. Most liner materials can be cut and solvent-welded to fit odd-shaped water features.

Another option is a fiberglass pool shell—think of it as a spa buried in the ground and filled with plants and fish. A number of shapes and sizes are available, but many are too shallow to house fish. Though these cost more than PVC pools, life expectancy is longer—more than 20 years.

Freeform concrete can be stacked to a slope of about 45 degrees with ordinary mix and can be made steeper with an air-sprayed, professionally applied mixture called gunite or shotcrete. For crisp perpendicular angles and perpendicular walls, you'll need carpentered forms with poured concrete. The material is normally reinforced with steel to withstand the pressure of soil and water.

For fast, inexpensive masonry construction, it's hard to beat concrete blocks; for a warmer appearance, veneer them with brick, stone, tile, or plaster. Plan to treat blocks with two coats of a cement-base waterproofing compound or another membrane before veneering.

Pumps, Pipes & Filters

A simple pool pump can supply a stream, waterfall, or fountain; aerate the water; and power a filter system. Pumps come in two basic types: submersible and recirculating. The best submersible pumps are made from brass and stainless steel; housings coated with epoxy resin are also popular. These pumps are designed for low-volume, part-time use. If the volume of water is large and demand is constant, choose a recirculating pump housed outside the pool. Don't buy the energy-gobbling swimming-pool design; instead, look for a circulator pump, which moves more water at lower pressure.

Filters for garden pools run a gamut from simple strainer baskets to swimming-pool filters to custom-built biological filters for large koi ponds. For a small garden pool that has no plants or fish, chemical filtration—using algicides and other water-clearing agents—is often the best choice.

Installing a drain in your pool makes maintenance easier. If you need to keep a constant water level, install a float valve—either a special pool model or the toilet-bowl type.

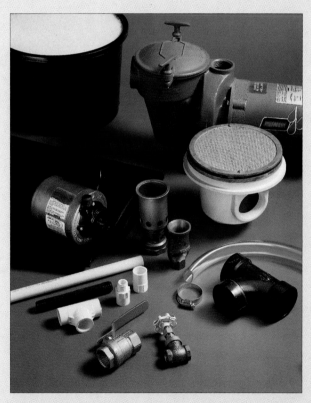

Pool hardware comes in many sizes and capacities. Basic fittings and valves are at front; submersible pump, flexible liner, fountain jets, and drain hold down center stage. Looming in background are in-line biological filter (left) and heavy-duty circulator pump (right).

CONCRETE

Though often typecast as cold and forbidding, poured concrete is even more adaptable than brick. Used with the proper forms and reinforcement, it can conform to almost any shape. It can be lightly smoothed or heavily brushed, surfaced with colorful pebbles, swirled, scored, tinted or painted, patterned, or molded to resemble another material. And if you get tired of the concrete surface later on, you can use it as a foundation for a new pavement of brick, stone, or tile set in mortar.

Shopping for Concrete

Concrete is a mixture of portland cement, sand, aggregate, and water. Cement is the "glue" that binds everything together and gives the finished product its hardness. The sand and aggregate (usually gravel) act as fillers and control shrinkage.

If your project is fairly large, ordering materials in bulk and mixing them manually is the economical way to go. Buying bagged, dry ready-mixed concrete is expensive, but it's also convenient, especially for small jobs. On a grander scale, a commercial transit-mix truck can deliver enough concrete to fill forms in a single pour.

Exact formulas of concrete vary from area to area, depending on local climate, season, and materials. In areas with severe freeze-thaw cycles, you'll need to add an air-entraining agent to prevent cracking. Be sure to ask your supplier about the best formula for your needs. If you're using ready-mixed, figure about .37 cubic yards of concrete for every 10 cubic feet.

To locate concrete plants, look in the Yellow Pages under "Concrete—Ready-Mixed."

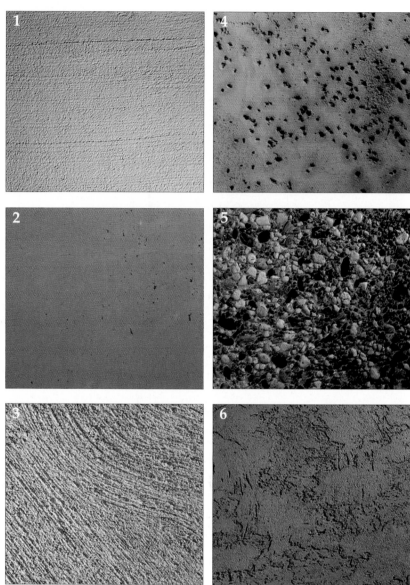

Shown above are six basic concrete finishes. Semismooth texture (1) is achieved with a wooden float. Slick troweled surface (2) is suitable for covered patios. Broomed surface (3) is best where maximum traction is needed. Rock salt (4), exposed aggregate (5), and travertine (6) are three popular decorative finishes.

Concrete needn't be poured in boring rectangles. The "freeform" pads at right act like giant stepping-stones, help integrate patio and walks into naturalistic garden design. Like concrete at top of facing page, pads are topped with exposed aggregate.

Classic aggregate paving surrounds a swimming pool, teamed with wood decking along rear slope. Surface pebbles may be plain or colored, added to basic concrete mix or floated on a later top coat. Control joints add visual interest and relieve slab stress.

Surface Treatments

Concrete pavings are typically given some type of surface treatment, both for appearance's sake and to provide traction.

You can wash or sandblast concrete to uncover the aggregate. Or embed colorful pebbles and stones in it (this finish, generally known as exposed aggregate, is probably the most popular contemporary paving surface). Larger river rocks and fieldstones can also dress up a dull slab.

Other ways to modify the standard steel-troweled concrete surface include color-dusting, staining, masking, sandblasting, acid-washing, and salt-finishing. A professional can also stamp and tint concrete to resemble stone, tile, or brick. The patterns simulate either butted joints or open ones, which can then be grouted to look like unit masonry.

Combining concrete and brick is popular; and tile and flagstone are other materials that complement concrete. Wood, steel, or copper dividers can be used to act as control joints to help prevent cracking. These materials also allow you to divide the job into smaller, more manageable pours.

Creating a Softer Look

Several techniques can allow concrete to be used pleasingly in a more casual environment. The surface treatments discussed earlier are a good start; coloring, texturing, or stamping make concrete look more natural. You can also leave planting pockets in a freshly poured slab, then fill them with soil and plants. Drip tubing can be routed to these pockets to water planted areas without soaking the paving.

Or dig holes or shape curved forms and fill them with concrete. The resulting pads—with planting spaces in between—can be smoothed, textured, or seeded with aggregate.

LANDSCAPE DESIGNER: NICK WILLIAMS & ASSOCIATES

DESIGN: ROGERS GARDEN

Concrete can be colored, textured, or stamped to resemble a number of other materials. The multihued walkway at left has the look of aged slate tiles, but is actually top-colored, embossed, and chemically stained concrete. Fish-scale pattern above is one of many concrete stamping possibilities; spaces between scales may be left open or grouted.

Blue concrete river meanders throu side-yard patio, past fragment islands in a gray field. A band of da blue ceramic tiles accents the bac ground. Some areas of concrete smooth, while others are scor and brush

CONCRETE PAVERS

Available in many sizes, colors, and textures, concrete pavers are no longer limited to the 12-inch squares you've seen for years. Shapes include circles, rectangles, and puzzle-like contours that interlock. Very easy to install, pavers are an ideal material for do-it-yourselfers.

Paver Types

A simple square can be part of a grid or even a gentle arc. Squares or rectangles can butt together to create broad unbroken surfaces, or they can be spaced apart and surrounded with grass, a ground cover, or gravel for textural interest.

Interlocking pavers fit together like puzzle pieces. Made of extremely dense concrete that is pressure-formed in special machines and laid in sand with closed (butted) joints, they form a surface more rigid than brick. No paver can tip out of alignment without taking several of its neighbors with it; thus, the surface remains intact even under very substantial loads. Interlocking pavers are available in tan, brown, red, and natural gray, plus blends of these colors.

Modern cobblestone blocks are very popular for casual gardens; butt them tightly together and then sweep sand or soil between the irregular edges.

Turf blocks, a special paver variant, are designed to carry light traffic while retaining and protecting ground-cover plants. These suggest the possibility of grassy patios and driveways, and can create side-yard access routes that stand up to wear.

Concrete "bricks," available in classic red as well as imitation "used" or antique, are increasingly popular as substitutes for the real thing; and in many areas, they're significantly less expensive.

What about the Site?

Beneath the pavers, you'll need a 1½- to 2-inch base of construction sand—and in colder climates or for pavings doubling as driveways—a deeper sub-base of crushed gravel and filter fabric (see drawing on page 18). Be sure to plan adequate drainage and grade.

You can let pavers merge with the surrounding landscape, but containing them within edgings will help prevent shifting. Since edgings are installed first, they also serve as good leveling guides for preparing the base and laying the pavers.

Shopping for Pavers

Different-size circles, squares, and rectangles can be found at most building and garden supply centers. Availability may vary depending on location. Some interlocking shapes are proprietary, available at only a few outlets or direct from distributors. To locate these, check the Yellow Pages under "Concrete Products."

Precast pavers include "stepping-stones" (far left), "brick" patterns, and interlocking types (center). Custom-made pavers

Elegant interlocking pavers, set in sand, blend smoothly with aggregate steps. Fixed edgings, set in mortar or concrete, maintain clean lines while securing field units.

(near right) imitate adobe, stone, and Saltillo tiles. Turf block (far right) allows for grassy patios or driveways.

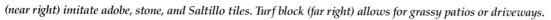

CONCRETE

PAVERS

What appear to be used bricks are actually brand-new pavers, creating a circular entry patio. Field pavers are laid in sand in herringbone pattern, ringed by tightly butted edging course with wood chip borders beyond.

Paver cost is determined by size and texture; for example, a 1½-inch-thick 12-inch square of plain or colored concrete costs about $1; seeded with an aggregate of pebbles, the same-size paver costs $3.40. Custom systems may cost from $5 to $8 per square foot.

Some landscape professionals cast their own pavers in custom shapes, textures, and colors: adobe, stone, and imitation tile, for example. You can also make your own pavers, though they won't be as strong as standard pressure-formed units.

Be cautious when choosing colored concrete pavers. The pigment in some is very shallow, and bare concrete may show through deep scratches or chips.

LANDSCAPE DESIGNER: DON WIHLBORG

Geometric pattern with gray border courses is set atop base of filter fabric and packed gravel. Pressure-treated wooden edgings help lock patio in place.

Large square pavers form a sturdy but user-friendly garden platform. Stepped edgings bridge hardscape and garden, form interesting pathway lines.

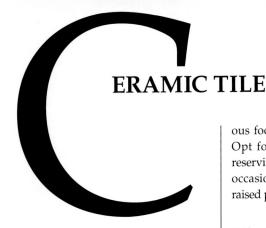

CERAMIC TILE

Tile works well in both formal and informal garden situations. Its earthy brown and red tones blend with natural colors outdoors, and the hand-fired pigments are permanent and nonfading. Because tile looks great indoors, too, it's a good flooring choice for an indoor room that relates to a patio as well as for the patio itself.

Glazed or Unglazed?

Glaze is a hard finish, usually colored, applied to the clay surface before final baking. Most bright, flashy tiles you see in tile displays are glazed.

Unless a special grit is added to glazed tiles, they can make treacherous footing when wet. The solution? Opt for unglazed tiles for paving, reserving the colorful glazed tiles for occasional accents or for edgings or raised planting beds.

Tile Types

Most outdoor tile falls into one of three categories: pavers, quarry tile, or synthetic stone.

Pavers are made by pouring the clay into wooden or metal molds, removing the molds, drying or curing the tiles, and then firing them. They usually have a grainy, handcrafted look. Perhaps the best-known hand-molded pavers are Saltillo tiles (named for the city in Mexico where they are made). It's best not to use pavers outdoors in cool, wet climates, where mildew and moss are likely to become problems.

Quarry tiles are denser and more regular in shape than pavers. They come glazed or unglazed, in natural shades of yellow, brown, and red. These tiles are made by squeezing clay into forms under great pressure, then firing them until they're quite hard. They're available with rounded edges and in corrugated finishes.

Synthetic stone is now being developed by tile manufacturers impressed by the increasing popularity of real stone. These tiles, which mimic the look of granite and sandstone, generally have enough surface bite to be used on patios. Colors include black and various shades of gray and beige.

What about price? You may pay as little as $1.30 to $2.25 per square foot for Mexican Saltillos and as much as $15 for some French pavers. Quarry tiles and machine-made glazed tiles run from about $3 up to $12 per square foot. To find outlets, look in the Yellow Pages under "Tile—Ceramic, Dealers."

Earth-toned ceramic tiles may look similar, but they have quite different properties. Shown from left to right: hand-molded, unglazed; machine-made, unglazed; machine-made, glazed; and concrete imitations.

Saltillo tiles wrap around the spa and lead down the steps beyond a graceful, multilevel patio. Irregularities and white efflorescence are considered part of the charm of this hand-molded material.

DESIGN: BERTOTTI LANDSCAPING, INC.

Tiles come in a rainbow of styles and colors, but be sure they're suitable for paving before buying. Hand-painted tiles (right) form colorful accents to flagstone stair treads, but are often too slick for overall paving. Synthetic stone tiles (below), fired from hard porcelain, are an elegant option. Here, they form slip-resistant surround for swimming pool and spa.

LANDSCAPE DESIGNER: MICHAEL GLASSMAN/ENVIRONMENTAL CREATIONS

There's no law against having fun with tile. This salamander detail was fashioned from tile shards set in mortared background.

Installation Options

Heavy tiles that are at least ¾ inch thick can be laid in a ½-inch sand bed; extra sand or soil locks joints together and allows plantings to gain a foothold.

However, the most stable bed for any tile is a 1-inch mortar bed over an existing concrete slab or a newly poured one. Lay the tiles, leaving ⅜- to ½-inch open joints (the more uneven the units, the bigger the space should be), and fill the joints with grout in a complementary or contrasting color.

To Seal or Not to Seal?

Some unglazed tiles are sealed at the factory. Unsealed, unglazed units should be sealed with a penetrating sealer (it allows the tile to "breathe") after installation.

A sealer may darken the tile's surface or give it a shiny appearance, so you may wish to test it first. Ask your tile dealer to recommend the sealer most appropriate for your situation.

ADOBE:
A touch of the old Southwest

Few materials can give a quality of rustic ease to a garden the way adobe does. Spaced with 1-inch open joints, adobe creates a living floor; low-growing plants and moss fill the joints, softening the look (and feel) of the area paved.

Historically, adobe structures were doomed to decay, victims of the combined forces of summer heat and winter rain. Today, however, adobe is made with an asphalt stabilizer that keeps the bricks from dissolving.

Although found mainly in Arizona, New Mexico, and Southern California, adobe can be used effectively almost anywhere in the country. Outside the West, though, delivery charges can make it quite costly.

Laying adobe in sand allows for good drainage and extends the life of the blocks. Use a 2-inch sand bed, but be sure it's completely level. If you allow blocks to straddle humps or bridge hollows, they may break. Railroad ties form rustic edgings while holding sand and blocks in place.

The most common block size is 4 by 7½ by 16 inches. But because the dimensions of blocks vary slightly, it's usually difficult to lay them in patterns that call for tight fitting. Leave 1-inch open joints between units and scoop out or fill in sand as necessary to compensate for irregularities.

Running bond, jack-on-jack, and basket-weave patterns (see page 74) all work well, and the latter two require no cutting. If you do need to cut adobe, however, it's easy to do with a sledge and brick set, or with an old saw.

Fill the joints with sand or soil. Filling with soil permits crevice planting, which eases the look. Use mortar only when it's essential: manufacturers have found that adobe failure often starts at mortar joints.

Sizes and shapes of adobe blocks vary with location of maker. Lay blocks in a sand bed with open joints; fill joints with more sand or with soil for plantings.

STONE

Stone pavings have the appeal of a thoroughly natural material, and most are very durable. Flat flagstones and cut stone are ideal for formal paving. For a more informal look, you can use irregularly shaped rocks and pebbles, setting them on soil or in concrete.

Marble and granite are igneous (volcanic) rock, and create the hardest surfaces. Sandstone, limestone, and other sedimentary stones are more porous; they usually have a chalky or gritty texture. Dense, smooth slate is a fine-grained metamorphic rock. The availability of stone types, shapes, sizes, and colors varies by locale.

Flagstone

Technically, flagstone is any flat stone that's either naturally thin or split from rock that cleaves easily. The selection pictured at right below gives you an idea of the range of colors and textures available at masonry and building supply yards. Prices depend on where you live in relation to where the stone originates; for 1-inch-thick stone, averages range from $200 to $340 per ton (to cover 100 square feet). Expect natural color variations within each type of stone.

When selecting flagstone for outdoor paving, think of how it will be used. Formal entry and entertaining areas should be smooth surfaces, safely accommodating high heels. Patios that serve as sitting and dining areas also need a level surface for chairs and tables; select a stone with a fairly smooth surface. Although some lighter pink and tan Arizona flagstones have smooth surfaces, their porous texture (absorbing oils and stains) should be considered before they're placed under eating areas or near messy fruit trees.

To create a rustic feel, select stones with a varied surface texture and rounded edges. For steps and entries, choose stones with a gritty texture for traction when surfaces are wet.

Quartzite and some slates can be slippery in frosty weather and require scoring for safety.

You can set stone in mortar or in sand. Paving stones come in various thicknesses; the thinnest (also called veneer) range from ¼ to ¾ inch thick, and should be laid on a 4-inch ccon-crete base. For areas that may encounter heavy loads (such as driveways), use 1- to 2-inch stones.

Stone set in mortar looks best in formal, permanent installations; plan to lay it atop a concrete slab, as shown below. Laid in sand, stone can look pleasingly casual, especially when plants are used between the joints.

Stone Tiles

Many stone types are available precut in rectangular shapes. Some have random widths and thicknesses. Popular tiles include those made from slate, granite, adoquin (a dense volcanic stone), sandstone, and quartzite.

Stone tiles are usually laid in mortar with very thin grout lines, which gives them a more formal look.

Flagstones in Mortar

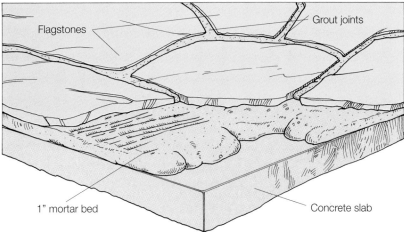

To support irregular flagstones firmly, start with a concrete slab—either new or existing. Then set stones in a 1-inch mortar bed. Finally, fill joints between stones with grout.

You'll find a good selection of random-

Sandstone paths, steps, and landings lead down to a circular patio made with tightly fitted stones and grout joints in complementary color.

size flagstones at most garden centers. We show ones most often used, but offerings vary by region—and by supplier.

Other Stones

Fieldstones, river rocks, and pebbles are less expensive than flagstone. These water-worn or glacier-ground stones produce rustic, uneven pavings that make up in charm for what they lack in smoothness underfoot. Price varies widely: a generic river rock may cost as little as $50 per ton; granite and other specialty stones can top $300.

Smaller stones and pebbles can be set in mortar or seeded into concrete; large stones may be laid directly on soil as raised stepping-stones. An entire surface can be paved solid with cobblestones set in concrete or tamped earth. Or use mosaic panels to break up an expanse of concrete, brick, or larger flagstones.

Some natural stones can become dangerously slick in wet weather. Because their shapes are irregular, they may be uncomfortable to walk on. It's best to confine such surfacing to a limited area.

Rectangular slate tiles are laid in an even grid, with matching grout between units. Because they're set in mortar, they don't require a separate edging to keep them in place. Note how tiles are cut around accent boulders.

LANDSCAPE ARCHITECT: LOUIS J. MARANO

LANDSCAPE ARCHITECT: THE BERGER PARTNERSHIP, P.S.

Stone presents a wide palette of shapes, colors, and textures. Square stone tiles (right), fashioned from Idaho quartzite, are tightly butted with impeccable grout lines. Mexican adoquin pavers (below) add color and texture to an open-air dining room. Mosaic sun pattern (bottom right), carefully fashioned from dark pebbles, forms focal point in lighter background.

LANDSCAPE ARCHITECT: RICHARD WILLIAM WOGISCH

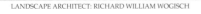

LIGHTING UP THE NIGHT

Safety, security, and decoration—all three are functions of outdoor lighting, and all can be achieved with a good lighting scheme. The only restriction is the need to keep both glare and wattage at a low level.

Low-voltage or Standard Current?

When it comes time to light up your landscape, you can choose a standard 120-volt system or use a low-voltage scheme. You have options in bulbs and fixtures for either plan.

Because they're safer, more energy efficient, and easier to install than standard 120-volt systems, low-voltage lights are often used outdoors. Such systems use a transformer to step down standard household current to 12 volts. Although low-voltage fixtures lack the "punch" of line-current fixtures, their output is sufficient for most outdoor applications.

But the standard 120-volt system still has some advantages outdoors. The buried cable and metallic fixtures give the installation a look of permanence,
light can be projected a great distance, and 120-volt outlets accept standard power tools and patio heaters.

Fixtures & Bulbs

Outdoor fixtures range from well lights and other portable uplights to spread lights that illuminate paths or bridges to downlights designed to be anchored to the house wall, eaves, or trees.

Most outdoor fixtures are made of bronze, cast or extruded aluminum, copper, or plastic. But you can also find decorative stone, concrete, and wood fixtures (redwood, cedar, and teak weather best). Sizes vary. When evaluating fixtures, look for gaskets, high-quality components at joints and pivot points, and locking devices for aiming the fixtures.

Choose the bulb and effect you want first and then the appropriate fixtures. Low-voltage halogen MR-16 bulbs are popular for accenting; PAR spotlights, available in both low and standard voltage, are best to light trees or wide areas.

Low-voltage systems include transformer, timer, and easy connections to small cables run on or just below the surface. Compact, innovative fixtures include uplights, downlights, and step lights in many styles.

120-volt lighting packs a bigger power punch but requires beefier components and extra safety measures. Boxes and fixtures must be sealed from weather, and wires are run via buried cable or in metal conduit.

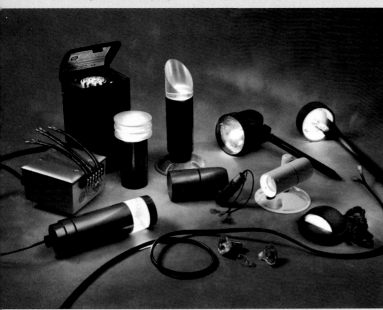

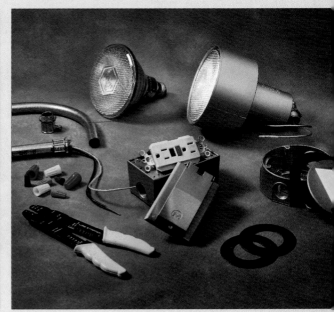

Basic Lighting Techniques

Path lighting

Moonlighting

Uplighting

Backlighting

Grazing

Silhouetting

Accenting

Less is Best

Because the contrast between darkness and a light source is so great, glare can be a big problem at night. Three rules of thumb are: choose shielded fixtures; place fixtures out of sight lines; and lower overall light levels.

With a shielded light fixture, the bulb area is protected by an opaque covering that directs light away from the viewer's eyes. Instead of a hot spot of light, the eye sees the warm glow of the lighted object.

Place fixtures out of sight lines, either very low (as along a walk) or very high. By doing that, you can direct them in such a way that only the light playing in the tree branches is noticed—not a bright glare.

Lower light levels by using several softer lights strategically placed around the patio and yard rather than one high-wattage bulb.

A little light goes a long way at night. Twenty watts is considered strong, and even 12 watts can be very bright. If you're using line current, choose bulbs with a 50-watt maximum.

For a look at basic lighting techniques, see the illustration above. On patios, low light levels are usually enough for quiet conversation or outdoor dining. Add stronger light for serving or barbecuing areas. Downlights are popular, but indirect lighting, diffused through plastic or another translucent material, is also attractive.

Illuminating foliage can be an effective way to combine functional and decorative lighting. Decorative mini-lights help outline trees and lend sparkle to your landscape. Placing the lights on separate switches and installing dimmers adds flexibility.

Strings of mini-lights are also useful for lighting steps, railings, and walkways. If your house has deep eaves or an overhang, consider weatherproof downlights that will illuminate use areas without the fixtures being visible.

Don't forget the view from inside. To avoid a "black hole" effect, strive to balance light levels on both sides of a window or French doors. Use soft light in the foreground, build up the middle ground, and save the highest wattage for the background.

LOOSE MATERIALS

For economy, good drainage, and a more casual look, consider including such materials as pea gravel, bark, or wood chips in your patio plan.

You needn't opt for the large, uninteresting expanses that give some aggregates a bad name. Gravel can be raked into patterns or used as a decorative element with other paving materials. You might use dividers to set off different colors and textures. Buy them by the bag (small jobs only), by the ton (gravel and other rocks), or by the cubic yard.

Wood Chips & Bark

By-products of lumber mills, wood chips and shredded bark are springy and soft underfoot, generally inexpensive, and easy to apply. You'll probably find a wide variety of colors and textures. To work successfully as patio surfaces, they should be confined inside a grid with headers.

Shredded bark, sometimes called gorilla hair, is the most casual of the loose materials. It compacts well and is useful as a transitional material between plantings.

Rock

Gravel is collected or mined from natural deposits. Crushed rock is mechanically fractured and then graded to a uniform size. If the surface of the rock has been naturally worn smooth by water, it's called river rock. Frequently, gravels are named after the regions where they were quarried.

When making a choice, consider color, sheen, texture, and size. Take home samples as you would paint

Loose paving materials are available by the sack or by the truckload. Shown from top to bottom are "gorilla hair" (shredded bark), redwood chips, decomposed granite, quartz pebbles, redrock, and river rock.

chips. Keep in mind that gravel color, like paint color, looks more intense when spread over a large area.

Crushed rock compacts firmly for stable footing on paths and walkways, but its sharp edges may hurt bare feet. Smooth river rock feels better, but tends to roll underfoot. Small river rock, also called pea gravel, is easiest to rake.

Crushed rock creates a comfortable, casual transition from patio to garden. As shown at right, rock areas may be shaped (here by curved rubber edgings) for striking contrasts in color and texture. Gravel garden floor shown below provides a low-maintenance base for a sitting area.

INDEX

Adobe, 60, 87
Aggregates, exposed. *See* Exposed aggregates
Amenities, 17
Architects, 20, 21
Atriums. *See* interior court-yards

Backyard sites, 8
Balcony sites, 8–9, 32, 46
Barbecues, 56–57
Bark, 94
Base map, 12–13
Benches, 16, 17, 49, 54, 67. *See also* Furniture
Brick
  edgings, 27, 33
  installation, 18, 74
  pathways, 27, 60
  patio designs, 26, 27, 31, 41, 43, 58, 60–61, 72, 73, 74
  patterns, 74
  shopping, 74
  sizes, 73
  steps, 44
  types, 72–73
  walls, 33
Building codes, 13, 19

Ceramic tile
  accents, 57, 62, 64, 65, 79, 86, 87
  finishes, 84
  installation, 87
  pathways, 79
  patio designs, 85, 86
  seals, 87
  shopping, 84
  types, 84–85
Circulation patterns, 15–16
Clearances, 16
Climate, 10–11
Codes. *See* Building codes
Color, 14
Coloring concrete, 18, 35, 42, 45, 78
Concrete
  edgings, 39, 60, 80, 81, 82, 83
  finishes, 76, 78
  formulas, 76
  installation, 18, 20
  pathways, 77, 78, 79, 83
  patio designs, 5, 6–7, 26, 29, 32, 33, 34. 36, 39, 40, 42, 51, 62, 77, 78, 79, 81, 82, 83
  resurfacing, 9
  shopping, 76, 80, 82
  slabs, 18
  steps, 40, 44, 45, 81
  techniques, 78
  walls, 28
Contour maps, 12–13
Contractors, 20, 21
Crushed rock, 94–95

Decks
  amenities, 17
  cantilevered, 28, 30, 42, 49

Decks *(cont'd)*
  designs, 8–9
  elevated, 4, 21, 32, 42, 46, 47, 55, 59, 67
  entry, 24, 34, 35, 69
  finishes, 71
  installation, 19, 25
  low-level, 24–25, 63, 68, 69
  materials for, 66–71
  multilevel, 8, 29, 32, 35, 39, 48, 67
  planning, 7–17, 19–21
  poolside, 30, 39, 62–63
  rooftop, 8, 42, 43
  wraparound, 8, 26
Deed restrictions, 12–13
Design elements, 14
Designs
  for entries, 1, 24, 34–35, 45, 69, 82
  for gazebos, 52–53
  for hillside lots, 28, 29, 30, 42, 46, 49, 67, 81, 89
  for large lots, 31, 39, 40, 48, 50, 51
  for narrow lots, 32, 33, 62, 79
  for outdoor rooms, 36–37, 50, 56–57, 91, 95
  planning, 6–18, 20–21
  for pools and spas, 6–7, 14, 22–23, 29, 38–39, 40–41, 43, 62–63, 68, 77, 85, 86
  for rooftops, 42–43
  for side yards, 9, 33, 62, 78
  for small lots, 32, 33, 60–61
Detached sites, 1, 5, 8, 30–31, 50, 52, 53, 89, 95
Draftspersons, 21
Drainage, 13, 17, 18
Driveways, reclaimed, 9, 35

Easements, 12
Edgings
  brick, 27, 33
  concrete, 39, 60, 80, 81, 82, 83
  installation, 18
  rubber, 95
  stone, 22–23, 35, 38, 59
  wood, 44, 66, 73
Entry spaces, 5, 9, 24, 34–35, 45, 69, 82
Exposed aggregates, 5, 29, 33, 44, 62, 76, 77, 78, 81

Fences, for wind control, 11
Fireplaces, 57
Flagstones. *See* Stone
Fountains. 6–7, 32, 33, 41, 53, 62
Furniture, 16, 17, 48–49. *See also* Benches

Gazebos, 41, 52–53
Grading, 16
Gravel, 18, 94–95

Hardware
  deck, 70, 71
  pool, 75
Heating, 57
Hillside lots. *See* Designs for hillside lots
Hot tubs. *See* Spas

Interior courtyards, 9, 33

Kitchens, outdoor, 56–57

Landscape architects, 16, 20, 21
Landscape contractors, 21
Landscape designers, 20, 21
Landscaping with plants, 11, 13, 14, 48, 31, 32–33, 43, 44, 49–50, 58–61, 93
Large lots. *See* Designs for large lots
Lighting, 44, 92–93
Loose materials, 18, 94–95
Low-level decks, 24–25, 63, 68, 69
Lumber, 66–71. *See also* Wood

Masonry. *See* Adobe; Brick; Ceramic tile; Concrete; Stone
Materials, 65–95
Microclimates, 10, 11
Modular decking, 25
Mortar, 74, 88
Movable spaces, 25, 33
Multilevel spaces, 8, 29, 32, 39, 43, 48, 67

Narrow lots. *See* Designs for narrow lots

Orientation, 10–11
Outdoor rooms, 36–37, 50, 56–57, 91, 95
Overheads. *See* Patio roofs

Pathways
  brick, 27, 60
  ceramic tile, 79
  concrete, 77, 78, 79, 83
  stone, 53, 89
  wood, 69
Patio-deck combinations, 28, 29, 34, 42
Patio roofs, 5, 10, 21, 27, 32, 36–37, 40, 41, 43, 50–53, 62, 77, 95
Patios
  amenities, 17
  detached, 6–7, 8, 22, 31, 38, 50, 52, 53, 83, 89, 95
  enclosed, 36–37
  entry, 9, 34, 35, 82
  installation, 20
  location, 8–11
  poolside, 6–7, 22–23, 29, 32, 38, 39, 43, 62, 77, 86
  rooftop, 42–43
  sites, 8–11
  wraparound, 8, 26–27
Pavers. *See* Ceramic tile; Concrete
Planning, 6–21
Plantings. *See* Landscaping with plants
Plant pockets, 31, 32, 59, 60, 78. *See also* Landscaping with plants
Pools, garden, 6–7, 22–23, 32, 62, 63, 68, 75
Poured concrete, *See* Concrete
Privacy, 14, 33, 34, 40, 41
Professionals, working with, 20, 21

Quarry tile. *See* Ceramic tile

Railings, 17, 39, 46–47, 48, 49, 59, 67,

Railroad ties, 44, 66, 73
Rain, 10
Raised beds. *See* Landscaping with plants
Retaining walls, 16–17, 22–23, 28, 34
Rocks, 30, 38, 94–95. *See also* Loose materials; Stone
Roofs, patio. *See* Patio roofs
Rooftop sites. *See* Designs for rooftops

Safety, 14, 46, 86
Sand beds, 18, 73, 74
Side-yard sites. *See* Designs for side yards
Sites, 8–11
Slabs. *See* Concrete
Slate. *See* Stone
Slide projector planning, 17
Small lots. *See* designs for small lots
Snow, 10
Soils engineers, 21
Spas, 1, 22–23, 30, 36, 39, 40–41, 62, 85, 86
Stamping, concrete, 18, 78
Steps, garden
  brick, 44
  ceramic tile, 85, 86
  concrete, 40, 44, 45, 81
  stone, 30, 62, 77, 86, 89
  wood, 35, 39, 40, 44, 49, 67
Stone
  edgings, 22–23, 35, 38
  installation, 88
  pathways, 53, 89
  patio designs, 14, 37, 22–23, 31, 50, 52, 53, 59, 61, 89
  steps, 30, 62, 77, 86, 89
  synthetic. *See* Ceramic tile
  tiles, 5, 88, 89
  walls, 14, 38
Storage, 54–55
Structural engineers, 21
Styles, 8–9
Subcontractors, 21
Sun, 10, 11
Sun-rooms, 9
Swimming pool surrounds, 9, 22–23, 29, 38–39, 43, 77, 86

Tile. *See* Ceramic tile; Stone tile
Tools, drafting, 13
Traffic patterns, 15–16
Tree wells, 23, 67

Use areas, 15

Walls, retaining. *See* Retaining walls
Water, landscaping with, 62–63
Weather, 10–11
Wheelchair access. *See* Wood, ramps, wheelchair
Wind, 10, 11
Wiring. *See* Lighting
Wood. *See also* Decks
  benches, 17, 48–49, 54, 67
  chips, 82, 94
  installation, 19
  railings, 46–47, 48, 49, 59, 67
  ramps, wheelchair, 17
  steps, 35, 39, 40, 44, 49, 67